In *The Authenticity Compass*, Pamel[a Bond's ...] and personal experience combined [with ...] perspectives to provide the reader w[ith ...] The scope of the approach is releva[nt to ...] interactions. This volume assists the reader in developing an introspective understanding of her or his preferred decision-making and problem-solving strategies and where these may lead to blind spots in addressing a host of professional as well as personal dilemmas. The reader participation approach facilitates the reader's likelihood to develop insight and increases the opportunity to assimilate and utilize the Compass in everyday circumstances. The work is relevant to individuals seeking to enhance their understanding of themselves and their ability to effectively manage, communicate, and interact with others.
—Richard H. Myers, PhD, scientist, psychologist, board-certified medical geneticist

Bond is a longtime student and practitioner of authentic living. Her book is not a check-the-box list of steps to success. Rather, it is a deeply reflective guide to making a positive difference in the world—a difference that is found at the intersection of personal authenticity and choice. This work is a thought-provoking read for anyone in search of a fulfilled and satisfying life that comes only when one follows one's Authenticity Compass.
—Gloria Ashby, teacher, coach, vice president of Fidelity Investments (retired)

Bond applied insight, deliberation, courage, and directions for living life to the fullest. The book is a ten-year journey filled with experiences, stories, and facts that align with skills and a compass to strengthen standards of service and mental fitness. Character, honesty, wisdom, and intellectual curiosity lead to functionality in government, academia, the media, and business. Bond will show you the way. *The Authenticity Compass* is a must-read book.
—Diane DiPiero-Saia, MS, MBA, professor, radio and television host

Pam Bond's extensive study, research, experience, and passion for the subject of authenticity have resulted in a fantastic work that provides tools and hope for the individual and the planet. I have been awed by how Pam Bond has managed multiple catastrophic challenges in her life and, in the words of Eleanor Roosevelt, "readjusted" ... while maintaining the essence of the joyous person I met many years ago. Over the course of our decades-long friendship, I have benefited from Pam's expertise. Now, having read her book, I understand the source of her wisdom and am excited to apply *the Authenticity Compass* more formally to my own life."
—Leonida Rasenas, MD

The Authenticity Compass is the achievement of Pamela Bond's purpose, to share with the world what she has learned in both work and living. Her synthesis and creative extension of the work of Deming and Jung for individuals and organizations offers both inspiration and a road map for awareness, responsible choices, and action in life. What a gift for us all!
—Vicki E. Beggs, PhD, psychologist

Bond's book, *The Authenticity Compass*, gives the user a great framework to aid in the identification and development of your organization's culture. The abundance of exercises makes this tool priceless when it comes to focusing on the value and spirit of teamwork in driving the right behaviors in your organization. Building trust and collegiality in any organization is an elusive critical success factor ... where consulting with each other in solving difficult and complex problems is a sign of strength and not weakness. Creating this type of culture takes time and discipline. This book has sound guidance for taking a deep dive into your organization's behavior metrics.
—Gregory J. Gailius, independent board director, PwC Deals Partner (retired)

THE AUTHENTICITY COMPASS

ESSENTIAL GUIDANCE FOR SUSTAINABLE SUCCESS

Pamela Bond

BALBOA.PRESS
A DIVISION OF HAY HOUSE

Copyright © 2020 Pamela Bond.

All rights reserved. No part of this book may be used or reproduced by any means, graphic, electronic, or mechanical, including photocopying, recording, taping or by any information storage retrieval system without the written permission of the author except in the case of brief quotations embodied in critical articles and reviews.

Balboa Press books may be ordered through booksellers or by contacting:

Balboa Press
A Division of Hay House
1663 Liberty Drive
Bloomington, IN 47403
www.balboapress.com
844-682-1282

Because of the dynamic nature of the Internet, any web addresses or links contained in this book may have changed since publication and may no longer be valid. The views expressed in this work are solely those of the author and do not necessarily reflect the views of the publisher, and the publisher hereby disclaims any responsibility for them.

The author of this book does not dispense medical advice or prescribe the use of any technique as a form of treatment for physical, emotional, or medical problems without the advice of a physician, either directly or indirectly. The intent of the author is only to offer information of a general nature to help you in your quest for emotional and spiritual well-being. In the event you use any of the information in this book for yourself, which is your constitutional right, the author and the publisher assume no responsibility for your actions.

Myers-Briggs Type Indicator, Myers-Briggs, MBTI and MBTI Logo are trademarks or registered trademarks of the MBTI Trust, Inc., in the United States and other countries.

All images and tables are the exclusive property of
The Authenticity Compass, LLC.

Print information available on the last page.

ISBN: 978-1-9822-5094-2 (sc)
ISBN: 978-1-9822-5096-6 (hc)
ISBN: 978-1-9822-5095-9 (e)

Library of Congress Control Number: 2020913090

Balboa Press rev. date: 11/18/2020

This book is dedicated to those who know that personal, organizational, and global truth must be in harmony for future generations to succeed.

CONTENTS

Acknowledgments xiii

Introduction xv

Chapter 1: Authenticity Compass (AC) Basics 1
    Why Mental Functions Are Important: The PJ Framework 2
        Exercise 1. Discovering Your Preferences 5
    Understanding Preferences 8
    A Methodology for Successful Behavior: The PDCA Skill Sets 10
    The AC: Linking Mental Functions to Skill Sets 12
        Exercise 2. Creating Your Authenticity Compass 13
        Exercise 3. Examining Your Authenticity Compass 16
    The ABCs of Authenticity 17
    Chapter 1 Takeaways 18

Chapter 2: Alignment 21
    Essential Skill Development 22
        Exercise 4. Group Alignment 23
    PDCA Cycles and Systems Thinking to Promote Alignment 24
        Exercise 5. Applying the PDCA Cycle 32
    The Importance of Stress Management 34
        Exercise 6. Present Life Experience Profile (PLEP) 35
    Chapter 2 Takeaways 40

Chapter 3: Balance 43
    Understanding Key Factors Influencing Balance 46
        Exercise 7. Establishing Mindfulness 54
    Balancing Your Dominant Energy: Four Stories 55
        Exercise 8. Spotting DQ Imbalance 65
    Chapter 3 Takeaways 66

Chapter 4: Choice **69**
   Choosing Alignment and Balance: Four Examples 73
   Learning to Live Without Regret 81
      Exercise 9. Your Legacy 83
   Creating Your Best Life: Awareness and Action 86
      Exercise 10. The SNTF Analysis: Increasing Self-
      Awareness 86
   The SElf-Examination (SEE) Method: Making Awareness-
   Fueled Choices 89
      Exercise 11. The SEE Method: Increasing Behavioral
      Awareness 93
      Exercise 12. Putting Positive Change in Motion 95
   Chapter 4 Takeaways 98

Chapter 5: Personal Success **101**
   Committing to Personal Authenticity 104
      Exercise 13. Your Pathway to Authenticity 104
   Identifying Your Authenticity Compass Success Factors 108
   Optimizing Your Success 114
      Exercise 14. Creating Your Plan for Success 116
   Chapter 5 Takeaways 118

Chapter 6: Authenticity Compass Applications **121**
   Application 1: Blind Spot Management 121
      How to Identify Your Blind Spot 122
      Exercise 15. Blind Spot Investigation 124
   Application 2: Relationship Harmony 126
      Minimizing and Eliminating Conflict 128
      Increasing Your Interaction Effectiveness 134
      Exercise 16. Promoting Relationship Harmony 137
   Application 3: The Backward-4 Method for Decision-Making ... 139
      Guideline Questions for Backward-4 Decision-Making 140
      Exercise 17. Decision-Making Using the Backward-4
      Method 142
   Application 4: ICE-ing (Identify/Cope/Exit-ing) 144

Exercise 18. Using ICE-ing to Return to Alignment
and Balance 146
Chapter 6 Takeaways 147

Chapter 7: Global Success **151**
Worldwide Problems Require Global Solutions 152
A Framework to Strengthen Global Collaboration 154
Using the Authenticity Compass to Improve Nations 159
Individuals Are the Heart of Global Success 162
The Authenticity Movement: A Vision for the Future 164
Closing Thoughts and a Call to Action 167

Notes **173**
Bibliography **177**
About the Author **181**
Note from the Author **183**

LIST OF FIGURES

Figure 1. The Perception-Judgment (PJ) Framework 2

Figure 2. The PDCA Cycle of Success 11

Figure 3. The Authenticity Compass 12

Figure 4. Your Personal Authenticity Compass 14

Figure 5. Promotion of Active Listening in Cycles of Success 26

Figure 6. Present versus Future Focus of AC Quadrants 28

Figure 7. Your AC and the Four Rooms 38

Figure 8. Maslow's Hierarchy of Needs 47

Figure 9. How Your Life Story Develops over Time 90

Figure 10. The Scholar Blind Spot Example 123

Figure 11. The Backward-4 Method for Decision-Making 140

LIST OF TABLES

Table 1. Preference Table A 6

Table 2. Preference Table B 6

Table 3. Authenticity Compass Quadrant (ACQ) Characteristics 15

Table 4. SNTF Analysis: Pre- and Post-SEE Method 93

Table 5. Strengths and Skill Development Opportunities by DQ 112

Table 6. Promoting Alignment, Balance, and Success 115

Table 7. Why Your Go-To Behaviors May Not Produce Desired Results 125

Table 8. Interpersonal Conflict Summary for Adjacent DQs 129

Table 9. Conflicts of Opposing Dominant Quadrants (DQs) 134

Table 10. SNTF Analysis: DQ Influence on Decision-Making 142

Table 11. The Universal Golden Rule 169

ACKNOWLEDGMENTS

IT IS WITH RESPECT AND heartfelt gratitude that I acknowledge my cousin and contributing editor, Sheila V. Brennan, for providing me with invaluable feedback and editorial assistance. Your opinions and suggestions helped shape this book. I am, and will be, forever grateful for your belief in my work and your demonstrated commitment to bringing it to the world. Your passionate desire to get *The Authenticity Compass* into the hands of others and your time-intensive commitment to the editing process made the publication of this book possible.

I also want to express my heartfelt thanks to the medical professionals who have given me exceptional care. Specific thanks goes out to my primary care physicians, Dr. Lini Bhatia and Dr. Holly Thomas; my rheumatologists, Dr. Robert Sands and Dr. Youmna Lahoud; my oncologist, Dr. Roberta Falke; and Bette Kisner, APRN-BC, MSN. Lastly, in the category of medical acknowledgements, I must thank Dr. Geoffrey Van Flandern for replacing my knees, Dr. Lifei Guo for giving me back the use of my right hand, and Dr. James Phillips for my new right hip. Saying I am grateful for your surgical skills is an understatement. I often think about how lucky I was to have had you as my surgeons.

Lastly, it is with pride that I thank my husband, Julian, and my children, Brittany, Ian, and stepdaughter, Heather, for their continual encouragement. Your love defines my life. There are many others who deserve credit for influencing the writing of this book. It is impractical for me to attempt to list them all because the list would be too long. Instead, let me give one big shout-out of thanks. Collectively, you taught me that truth and success walk hand in hand.

INTRODUCTION

THE AUTHENTICITY COMPASS GUIDES YOU to create a successful life by teaching you how to be true to yourself and those with whom you interact. It was developed by applying the large body of evidence-based research launched by the work of the well-known psychiatrist, Dr. Carl Jung, and W.E.Deming, an engineer known for his continuous improvement expertise.

My desire to understand how people achieve sustainable success began as a child witnessing the constant conflict in my parents' marriage. When I was fourteen, my mother died, leaving me with difficult questions. In my decades-long quest for answers, I pursued many areas of study, including the life sciences, mind-body medicine, information management, personality profiling, and positive psychology. Eventually, I found solid closure in the work done by Jung and Deming. Their research taught me certain key facts that determine the quality of human life, especially the interpersonal dynamics that support relationship harmony. Jung created a framework for exploring personal truth, and Deming provided direction for managing organizational truth. Both men dedicated their lives to understanding the relationships that exist between human perception, judgment, behavior, and success. Their work inspired the creation of the Authenticity Compass.

The concepts the Authenticity Compass applies are proven and time-tested. Everyone who uses the Authenticity Compass (AC) is encouraged by its immediate applicability to their lives. Being AC-literate is an ongoing process. This is because our physical, spiritual, thinking, and emotional lives are dynamic (i.e., change is constant). So while you will gain immediate insight from understanding the function of your Authenticity Compass, you learn you make your best choices by regularly evaluating your circumstances using it. Exercises are included in the book to reinforce the importance of regular, honest self-examination using your AC.

I believe an evolution in human consciousness is essential for humanity's long-term survival. Authenticity is a state of conscious awareness that enables you to make choices that align you with your world and support your physical, mental, emotional, and spiritual well-being. Expanding awareness of how you uniquely take in information from the world and how you process and react to that information creates your foundation for conscious choice. The Authenticity Compass encourages both self-awareness and the clarity of purpose required to engage cycles of success in each domain of your life. Developing individual authenticity establishes the cornerstones of family, group, business, and government success.

By employing proven principles, this book will help you:

- clarify your purpose, direction, and definition of success;
- develop skills that enable you to make the best possible choices; and
- establish the alignment and balance needed for your happiness and success.

How to Use This Book

This book takes you on a journey of self-discovery by providing exercises that build upon each other to increase your self-awareness. Follow these steps to derive the greatest benefit:

1. Take as much time as you need with each chapter and exercise. The book is designed to help you assess your present state and to take steps toward establishing your best life. This requires focus and a commitment to yourself.
2. Keep an Authenticity Compass journal to document your responses to the exercises and the insights they generate. You will likely do some of the exercises more than once, so keeping a journal will allow you to compare your results over time.

3. The material contained within this book reflects multiple disciplines and subdisciplines. You are encouraged to explore in more depth any areas that will strengthen your self-awareness.

Here is an overview of each chapter's contents:

- Chapter 1 positions you to begin your work with the Authenticity Compass by exploring your dominant and less-dominant skill sets.
- Chapter 2 examines the influence systems thinking, active listening, and stress management have on sustainable success. The chapter includes a Present Life Experience Profile (PLEP), a tool designed to strengthen personal alignment.
- Chapter 3 explores how physical, spiritual, mental, and emotional balance influence happiness. The chapter presents examples and exercises to help you uncover behaviors that may be inhibiting your happiness and success and positions you to address them.
- Chapter 4 illustrates the role your choices play in the development of your life story. The chapter discusses the pivotal relationships that exist between alignment, balance, and conscious choice. It presents the SEE Method for in-the-moment self-awareness and concludes with exercises for creating positive change.
- Chapter 5 encourages you to develop your pathway to personal success by optimizing your Authenticity Compass success factors. You will learn to cultivate a plan for alignment and balance based on your personal definition of success.
- Chapter 6 introduces you to a tool kit of four Authenticity Compass Applications that guide you to make conscious choices in the face of challenge. These are Blind Spot Management, Relationship Harmony, Backward-4 Decision-Making, and ICE-ing (Identify-Cope-Exit-ing).
- Chapter 7 asks you to consider some of the major challenges facing our planet; the importance of authentic action; and the roles individuals, organizations, and governments play in global success. The chapter looks at the work of established philanthropic organizations and discusses the need for

collaborative platforms, such as the Authenticity Compass, to support the health and welfare of all people. It concludes with a vision for the future of humanity that is defined by authenticity.

You are now ready to discover your Authenticity Compass, receive the benefits of its direction, and help establish a global authenticity movement focused on creating a harmonious, sustainable world.

CHAPTER 1
AUTHENTICITY COMPASS (AC) BASICS

UNDERSTANDING THE UNIQUE WAY IN which your mind functions and influences your behavior is key to promoting your happiness and success. How you view the world (your perceptions) and how you interpret this information (your judgments) directly influence the quality and direction of your life. By developing awareness of how your perceptions and judgments influence your behavior, the Authenticity Compass guides you to connect with your true self and make decisions that support your alignment and balance. In this chapter, you will learn the two components of the Authenticity Compass that create a foundation for positive change in your life:

- The Perception-Judgment *mental function framework* documents the fundamental drivers of human behavior.
- The PDCA Cycle of Success *behavioral framework* guides alignment, balance, and improvement in each domain of your life.

By connecting these two frameworks, the Authenticity Compass positions you to translate mental function and behavioral awareness into cycles of success. You will receive specific direction for employing your strongest skills and for developing those needed to overcome obstacles. The insights you obtain will bolster your sense of purpose, guide you in making conscious choices, and enable you to create your best life.

Why Mental Functions Are Important: The PJ Framework

To improve each choice you make, it is essential to be aware of the four mental functions that drive your choices and how your mind employs them.

First, your mind gathers information from the world (perceives) in two basic ways: through *sensing* (defined by facts) and by *intuition* (defined by beliefs). Then your mind processes this information (makes decisions) in two basic ways: using *thoughts* (defined by logic) and *feelings* (defined by concern for self and others). How and when these four mental functions develop directly influences the journey of your life. Dr. Carl Jung established the Perception-Judgment Framework using these four mental functions to explain the strengths, weaknesses, and differences in people's personalities and to demonstrate the role that mental functions play in one's experience of purpose and stability.

Figure 1. The Perception-Judgment (PJ) Framework

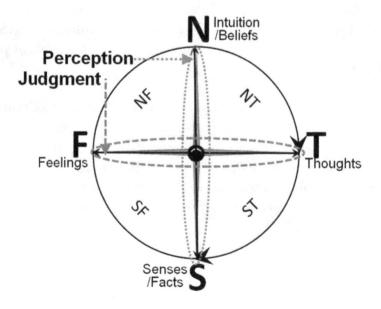

Figure 1 presents the *perception* and *judgment* axes as continuums that intersect to create four quadrants, the four perception-judgment (PJ) pairs:

- NT = Intuition ➜ Thinking
- ST = Sensing ➜ Thinking
- SF = Sensing ➜ Feeling
- NF = Intuition ➜ Feeling

It is essential that you understand that perceptions and judgments are always employed by the brain in perception-judgment (PJ) pairs. This means every time you take information in (perceive something), your mind also processes it (makes a judgment about it). So when you interact with your world, you are always using one of these four PJ pairs. For example, if you are caring for a baby, chances are you will be using your sensing-feeling PJ pair (SF). Likewise, if you are paying your bills, you are in a practical, results-oriented mode and will most likely employ your sensing-thinking PJ pair (ST). So while your brain employs only one PJ pair at a time, achieving success and happiness in life requires knowing how to make use of all four PJ pairs. Therefore, it is in your best interest to develop skills that support each pair.

What makes you unique is not just how you employ your mental functions of perception and judgment but that you have a dominant PJ pair you rely on more than the others. Jung's research shows that every person has an innate preference for how he or she perceives and judges the world. These findings were reinforced by Katharine Briggs and Isabel Myers, the mother-daughter team who created the Myers-Briggs Type Indicator (the MBTI) for psychological type based on Jung's work. So even though you may believe you use your senses and intuition equally to form your perceptions, it is not likely.[1] The same is true regarding how you form your judgments. You most likely have a preference, even if it is slight, for either feeling or thinking.

The first step in creating your Authenticity Compass is to identify the preferred PJ pair, which identifies your Authenticity Compass *dominant quadrant,* or DQ. Knowing how you tend to perceive and judge the world provides the basis for understanding the choices you make and the skills you may need to strengthen to experience balance and success in life.

Benefits you can expect to glean from identifying your DQ are:

1. **Identifying your strengths.** You are able to recognize why certain behaviors come naturally to you and why some skills are easier to learn and apply than others. The research of psychologists, neurobiologists, and other scientists indicates that the wiring of the brain differs based on mental function preference.[2] This means certain skills may be easier to learn and apply because of one's DQ. However, it does not mean skills that come naturally to one person cannot be learned by another and vice versa.
2. **Understanding growth opportunities.** You can more easily identify the skills you must develop to experience alignment and balance. Achieving your full potential requires developing the skills of all four Authenticity Compass quadrants, especially the skills of your less-dominant quadrants (LDQs). The quadrant directly opposite your DQ most likely describes the types of skills you are weakest in demonstrating (your blind spot). The quadrants adjacent to your DQ are also likely to be skill areas that require development.
3. **Decreasing stress.** You understand your reactions to stress more clearly. People usually respond to negative stress by employing their DQ skills. However, when desired outcomes are not achieved and situations remain charged, individuals are likely to rely on their LDQ skills. Using your Authenticity Compass in times of stress teaches you to identify the Authenticity Compass quadrant (ACQ) driving your behavior and apply the ACQ skills that can lessen your stress.
4. **Increasing relationship harmony.** You learn why it can be easy or difficult to interact with certain individuals. Typically, your easiest interactions are with people who share the same DQ as you. LDQ skill development will improve difficult interactions

The Authenticity Compass

that tend to occur with individuals whose DQ is opposite or adjacent to yours. You will learn how ACQ skill development can strengthen your interaction skills in chapter 5.

5. **Strengthening collaboration.** You obtain actionable insight for individual and group relationship development. Increased awareness and attention to DQ strengths and LDQ weaknesses improve team performance, increase relationship harmony, and strengthen collaborative decision-making. Chapter 5 covers applications that support these concepts.

Exercise 1. Discovering Your Preferences

In this exercise, you will identify your dominant PJ pair. This is dictated by whether your perception preference is for sensing (S) or intuition (N) and whether your judgment preference is for feeling (F) or thinking (T). If you have taken the MBTI, the middle two letters of your profile indicate your dominant PJ pair.

Instructions: Fill out the following two tables to help you determine the way you prefer to perceive and the way you prefer to judge your circumstances.

1. Lock into a completely relaxed and comfortable state.
2. Read the two items across each row, and check the *one* that most accurately describes your preferred mode of behavior. If neither choice feels appropriate, check nothing. If both choices seem appropriate, check both.
3. After completing each table, tally the check marks in the two columns. One column in each table should have more marks than the other, indicating a preference has emerged.
4. Use the Reveal Tables at the end of the exercise to determine the column header that identifies your preference (but please do not look ahead). If no preference emerges, use the suggestions provided at the end of the exercise.

Table 1. Preference Table A

Column 1	Column 2
__ I see what is.	__ I see what could be.
__ I describe facts first and then see the big picture.	__ I see the big picture first and then move to details.
__ I tend to focus on what works now.	__ I focus on how things could improve.
__ I like producing more than designing.	__ I like creating an idea more than acting on it.
__ I reach conclusions step-by-step.	__ I often leap to conclusions quickly.
__ I like many specific examples.	__ I prefer general concepts and few examples.
__ I prefer to focus on the immediate.	__ I like to focus on future possibilities.
__ I like to think sequentially.	__ I look for patterns, connections, themes.
__ I focus on and remember details.	__ I read for the main idea and skim naturally.
__ I am inclined to follow an agenda.	__ I like to use an agenda as a starting point.
___ Total number of check marks	___ Total number of check marks

Circle the column with more check marks (circle one):   **Column 1** or **Column 2**

Table 2. Preference Table B

Column 3	Column 4
__ I analyze to understand and use logic to decide.	__ I give personal values priority in decisions.
__ I am good at putting things in logical order.	__ I like harmony and strive for it.
__ I demand competence in myself and others.	__ Being accepted is important to me.
__ I have a talent for analyzing things.	__ I have a talent for understanding people.
__ I want things to be logical.	__ I want things to be pleasant.
__ I like to control the expression of feelings.	__ I express feelings with enthusiasm.
__ I ask why and need to understand why.	__ I trust others to help in good ways.
__ I tend to present goals and objectives first.	__ I tend to present points of agreement first.
__ I like to solve problems.	__ I like to help people.
___ Total number of check marks	___ Total number of check marks

Circle the column with more check marks (circle one):   **Column 3** or **Column 4**

The Reveal: Your Preference Table Results

Table A reveals your *perception preference*. So if you have more check marks in:

- ❖ Column 1, it is likely your perception preference is sensing, S

- ❖ Column 2, it is likely your perception preference is intuition, N

Please document your perception preference here (S or N)* _____

Table B reveals your *judgment preference*. If you have more checkmarks in:

- ❖ Column 3, it is likely your judgment preference is thinking, T

- ❖ Column 4, it is likely your judgment preference is feeling, F

Please document your judgment preference here (T or F)* _____

Combining results from Tables A and B, document your resulting preferred PJ pair:

(Either NT, NF, ST, or SF)*: _____

Again, these two letters will also designate your DQ (dominant Authenticity Compass quadrant), so commit them to mind for future use.

If no preference emerges: If you were not able to determine a result for one or both of the above tables, it is suggested that you do one of the following: a) redo the tables at a later time, b) look at the ACQ characteristics table near the end of this chapter and find the row with which you most closely identify and assume that is your DQ until such time you can determine it with more accuracy, or c) refer to the middle two letters of an MBTI assessment that you can obtain at www.cpp.com.

Understanding Preferences

Everyone has an innate preference for perceiving and judging information. Now that you have determined your PJ preferences, let's discuss what this means. Mental function preference is often explained by making an analogy to dominant hand preference. With tasks such as signing your name, you use your dominant hand because it is most comfortable to do so. Similarly, you tend to perceive and respond to circumstances in ways that are most comfortable for you. To strengthen your self-awareness, it is important to understand your preferences for using your mental functions.

Perception functions explain one's preference for taking in information from the world. A person who has a preference for sensing prefers to focus on facts, details, and the present whereas an individual who has a preference for intuition tends to focus on theories, possibilities, and the future.[3] Additionally, the following are often true:

People who prefer *sensing*[4] may:

- prefer to focus on the trees (details) rather than the forest (big picture)
- remember events as snapshots of what actually happened
- be practical and focused on the bottom line
- put trust in experience (not theory)
- miss new possibilities because they focus on the facts of the present or past

People who prefer *intuition*[5] may:

- prefer to focus on the forest (big picture) rather than on the trees (details)
- remember events by the impressions they made on them at the time
- solve problems through association or spontaneous insight
- like to do things that are new and different
- be unable to execute their ideas because they have not attended to the practical requirements

The *judgment functions* (thinking and feeling) explain one's preference for processing and making decisions about the information that one has perceived.

People who prefer *thinking*[6] may:

- gravitate toward technical or scientific careers
- notice inconsistencies easily
- only accept what they consider to be rational explanations
- believe it is more important to tell the truth than it is to be tactful
- miss the impact their logical decisions/actions have on others

People who prefer *feeling*[7] may:

- be seen as compassionate because they readily show their concern for people
- be strongly focused on creating harmony in their environment
- allow their hearts to rule their decisions
- believe it is more important to be tactful than it is to tell the whole truth
- be seen by others as indirect and idealistic because they prefer not to communicate the hard truth of situations

When thinking about the judgment mental functions, keep the following points in mind:

- ➤ *Judgment* does *not* mean *judgmental*. The judgment functions (thinking and feeling) enable individuals to come to conclusions and make decisions about the information they take in from the world (their perceptions). This is different than being judgmental, which means having critical or negative opinions, often without a basis in rational thought.
- ➤ *Feeling* does *not* mean *emotional*. An individual with a feeling preference tends to make decisions based on his personal values and the foreseeable affect his decisions will have on people. It does not mean that he is an emotional person or feels emotion

more deeply than someone with a thinking preference. Feelers tend to give more weight to personal and human concerns (the people issues) when faced with a decision.

> *Thinking* does *not* mean *smart*. Just because an individual prefers her thinking function over her feeling function it does not mean she has a higher IQ or is a better thinker than someone who prefers feeling. Thinkers simply tend to give more weight to objective principles and impersonal facts when making a decision.

Everyone uses all four mental functions. For example, all people with a sensing preference have intuitions, and all people with a preference for intuition rely on their senses. Similarly, all thinkers feel, and all feelers think.

Now that you are familiar with the first component of the Authenticity Compass (the Perception-Judgment cognitive framework) and have successfully identified your PJ preferences, let's explore how this translates to successful behavior. Understanding the four activities associated with the PDCA Cycle of Success and how these correspond to your PJ preferences is the next lesson.

A Methodology for Successful Behavior: The PDCA Skill Sets

Often referred to as the father of quality management, W. Edwards Deming (1900–1993) applied his knowledge of physics and statistics to establish a framework for successful human behavior known as the PDCA Cycle of Success. The PDCA Cycle is an improvement-focused framework made up of four interdependent activities: planning (*Plan*), execution (*Do*), monitoring/caretaking (*Check*), and inspired action/change management (*Act*). (See figure 2.) Each activity in the cycle represents an important skill set that requires balanced development and support.

Figure 2. The PDCA Cycle of Success

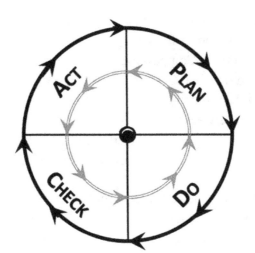

While everyone is capable of implementing each of the PDCA activities, it is likely that some of the skills required for the activities come more naturally to some individuals and groups than others. For example, in organizations that maintain world-class performance, each participating work group (and individual within it) knows its strength, who it depends on for information, and how it contributes to the success of the whole operation.

Deming committed his life to teaching the world that the PDCA Cycle is fundamental to the improvement of all processes, whether they exist in the workplace or in one's personal life. In fact, before his death, Deming maintained that to solve the man-made problems threatening our planet, world leaders must collaboratively embrace the feedback-driven management principles of the PDCA Cycle. Since World War II, the PDCA methodology has been adopted worldwide across essentially all industries. It has galvanized alignment in individual and group processes, from family units to global enterprises.

Your Authenticity Compass uses your PJ preference to point you to the PDCA activity/skill sets that are your natural strengths while highlighting the skill sets that may need further development.

The AC: Linking Mental Functions to Skill Sets

I studied and applied the work of Jung and Deming for many years before I realized the powerful synergy of their findings. As a result, I created the Authenticity Compass to provide a framework for individual, organizational, and global success management by combining Jung's PJ framework with Deming's behavioral model. Developing an awareness of the connection between your perceptions, judgments, and behaviors, you learn to harness your innate strengths and actualize cycles of success within your life and the organizations to which you belong.

As seen in figure 3, the poles of the Authenticity Compass correspond to the four mental functions Jung used to explain human experience. Each Authenticity Compass quadrant represents both a perception-judgment pair (NT, ST, SF, NF) and a corresponding PDCA activity. With awareness of how you use your mental functions and their related PDCA behavioral skill sets, you are positioned to make choices that strengthen your moment-to-moment alignment with the world and your sense of personal balance.

Figure 3. The Authenticity Compass

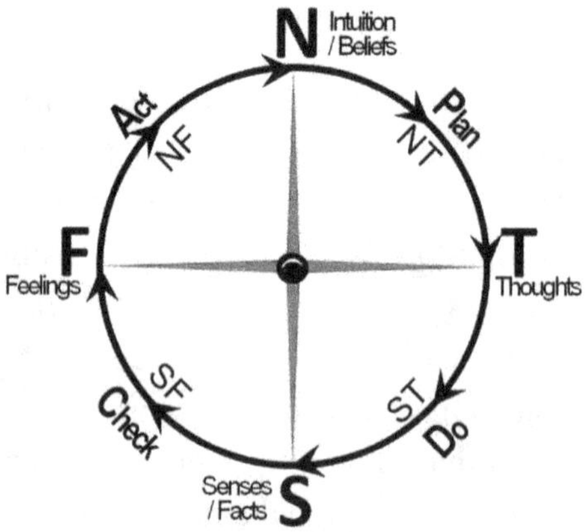

In the previous exercise, you identified your innate preferences for perception and judgment—your preferred PJ pair. You will now use this information to identify your DQ and create your Authenticity Compass.

Exercise 2. Creating Your Authenticity Compass

The purpose of this exercise is to create your Authenticity Compass, which involves identifying your dominant quadrant (DQ) and becoming aware of your three less-dominant quadrants (LDQs).

1. First, document the result of exercise 1, Discovering Your Preferences, on the line below:

   My preferred PJ pair: _____

2. Next, in the following list, find the row that contains your preferred PJ pair. Circle this row (i.e., the PJ pair, the PDCA activity that corresponds with it, and finally the dominant quadrant indicated at the end of the row). This is your DQ (Q1, Q2, Q3, or Q4).

PJ Pair (Jung)	PDCA Activity (Deming)	Dominant Quadrant
(NT) intuitive-thinking →	planning skills (Plan)	→ Q1
(ST) sensing-thinking →	execution skills (Do)	→ Q2
(SF) sensing-feeling →	caretaking skills (Check)	→ Q3
(NF) intuitive-feeling →	inspirational skills (Act)	→ Q4

3. Document your DQ, your preferred PJ pair, and its corresponding primary PDCA activity in your journal, and commit them to memory. This information is foundational to all the subsequent Authenticity Compass guidance you will receive from this book. Remember that all people have a dominant quadrant that influences their decisions and actions. All dominant quadrants are equally valuable.

4. Now, on the following diagram, shade in your dominant quadrant. Note that the remaining three ACQs are your LDQs. Copy this diagram into your journal.

Figure 4. Your Personal Authenticity Compass

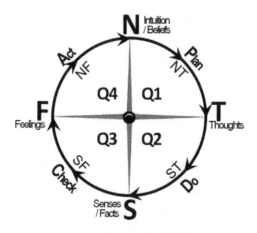

Congratulations on creating your personal Authenticity Compass! Your DQ describes your natural go-to energy and what is typically your strongest skill set. It is essential to understand that even though you have a DQ, your maturity as a human being requires you to:

A. Promote *balance* by developing skills that support each of the four ACQs.
B. Establish *alignment* by learning when the skills of a specific quadrant are needed.

For example, my DQ is Q1: intuitive-thinking (NT)/Plan. While I may be most comfortable employing the strategic planning skills of my DQ, I must regularly use skills of my less-dominant quadrants (Q2, Q3, and Q4) to effectively and appropriately respond to other people, changing situations, and my environment. I will admit it is not easy to develop skills associated with my less-dominant quadrants. However, the rewards of learning to interact in ways that help me better align with my environment and support my sense of personal balance are well worth the effort.

Because life's circumstances can frequently require you to rely upon your less-dominant quadrants, you must learn when and how to apply each of the four ACQ skill bases to experience growth as well as sustainable personal and professional success. So whether you consider the events

The Authenticity Compass

that take place during a twenty-four-hour period or over a much longer span of time (e.g., your adolescence, college years, married life, etc.), your maturity is linked to the skill development of all four AC quadrants. This is true even though learning certain skills may be challenging and feel unnatural to you. Jung describes mental function / skill development as one's path to maturity and wholeness. In Authenticity Compass terms, it means you are developing all four skill sets and learning to access each one as is needed in your life journey. Upcoming chapters will provide exercises to help you practice using these skills.

The following Authenticity Compass Quadrant Characteristics Table is provided to strengthen your knowledge of key characteristics associated with your DQ and those associated with your LDQs. This knowledge will become increasingly important to you as you work with your Authenticity Compass.

Table 3. Authenticity Compass Quadrant (ACQ) Characteristics

ACQ	Key Values	Defining Behavior	Skills (Typically Developed)	Common Positive Traits	Common Negative Traits
Q1 NT/Plan intuitive-thinking	Learning Mastery Control	Likes to design things. Focuses on how it all fits together	**Planning** **Designing**	Logical Ingenious "visionary"[8]	Controlling Overanalytical
Q2 ST/Do sensing-thinking	Results Duty Action	Likes to build and run things. Focuses on what is	**Building** **Implementing**	Matter-of-fact Practical "stabilizer"[9]	Too strict Impatient
Q3 SF/Check sensing-feeling	Stability Responsibility Harmony	Likes to be the caretaker ruler. Focuses on what matters to people	**Caretaking** **Monitoring**	Sympathetic Friendly "harmonizer"[10]	Manipulative Meddlesome
Q4 NF/Act intuitive-feeling	The Human Community Empowerment Innovation	Likes to inspire others. Focuses on what might be	**Inspiring others** **Motivating**	Enthusiastic Insightful "catalyst"[11]	Tendency to exaggerate Procrastinate

15

When looking at the table, remember the perception and judgment axes are continuums, so there are an infinite number of positions within the same quadrant. This means two people with the same DQ will often perceive, judge, and behave differently. For example, if you and a close friend both have a DQ of Q2 (sensing-thinking, ST/Do) and share the same circumstance, you will commonly report different experiences. The explanation is straightforward. You may have a stronger S preference than she does, and she may have a stronger T preference than you do (or vice versa).

Exercise 3. Examining Your Authenticity Compass

The skill sets you develop over your lifetime directly influence whether you experience alignment and balance. Answer the following questions to capture your initial reaction to your Authenticity Compass.

- Are you surprised by the characteristics and traits of your DQ, or do they make sense to you? Why?
- Now, look at your LDQs. Do you recognize any skill(s) that you could strengthen? Which skill(s)? If there are more than one, how would you prioritize them? Why?

The Authenticity Compass requires its users to assess the facts, beliefs, thoughts, and feelings influencing their behavior. As a result, they learn the roles self-awareness and conscious choice play in their ability to achieve and maintain

1. states of *alignment* within their relationships and life circumstances, and
2. mental, emotional, physical, and spiritual *balance*.

To master your life experience, you must recognize the facts and beliefs (i.e., the perceptions) influencing your thoughts and feelings (i.e., your judgments). This means being willing to identify any potential limiting beliefs that are influencing your perception of reality in order to consciously choose to focus on facts that support more life-affirming perceptions. Similarly, you must be able to articulate the thoughts and feelings currently defining any undesired behavior pattern in order to think, feel, and behave in new and different ways.

Using your Authenticity Compass supports developing your self-awareness and ultimately living consciously. But remember, while conscious living is conceptually straightforward, it requires effort, contemplation, and time to master. Self-reflection exercises such as the Present Life Experience Profile (PLEP, which is presented in chapter 2) are provided to help you enhance these skills. You are encouraged to engage your skills of self-awareness and conscious living by doing the exercises provided as frequently as you can until they become second nature. The ABCs of Authenticity are fundamental principles of the Authenticity Compass and are provided to assist you in this process.

The ABCs of Authenticity

Learning to employ these ABCs helps you avoid responding to life's challenges in ineffective and/or personally draining ways and instead live in a state of conscious awareness, alignment, and balance.

> **A = Alignment:** A state of optimum connection between two or more individuals, systems, or situations. It is established and sustained by the existence of a shared directed purpose. *Alignment is a prerequisite for sustainable success.*
>
> **B = Balance:** A state of equilibrium. Balance reflects strength and is expressed through mental, physical, spiritual, and emotional stability. Maintaining balance is how purpose is supported. *Balance is a prerequisite for sustainable happiness.*
>
> **C = Conscious Choice:** A decision focused on achieving alignment and balance. Conscious choice requires ongoing awareness of the internal forces (i.e., PJs, perceptions [senses/facts and beliefs], and judgments [thoughts and feelings]), and

external forces (e.g., social, environmental, economic, political) affecting an individual or a system. Conscious choice is the foundation for sustainable success and happiness.

Your Authenticity Compass encourages you to apply the ABCs of Authenticity to every aspect of your personal and professional life by reminding you that the states of alignment and balance are within your control. You can directly influence the quality of your life when you consciously choose how to view and react to each situation you face.

Chapter 1 Takeaways

- Each of us perceives the world using senses (based on facts) and intuitions (based on beliefs). We then process/judge the world with our thoughts and feelings. Jung's research showed that because these mental functions drive our behaviors, it is critical to be aware of how we use them.

- Each perception is always accompanied by a judgment (i.e., PJ pairs). There are four possible PJ pairs: NT, ST, SF, and NF. Your brain can only operate from one PJ pair at a time.

- The PDCA Cycle, defined by Deming, comprises the four behavioral skill sets needed to create and manage cycles of success: planning, doing, checking, and inspiring action.

- The Authenticity Compass connects the perception-judgment and PDCA frameworks so you can translate mental and behavioral awareness into success cycles. Each PJ-PDCA grouping defines an Authenticity Compass quadrant (ACQ). The four ACQs are:

    o **Q1**: NT/Plan: intuitive-thinking (the primary energy fueling *plan*ning activity)

- o **Q2**: ST/Do: sensing-thinking (the primary energy fueling *do*ing activity)
- o **Q3**: SF/Check: sensing-feeling (the primary energy fueling *check*ing activity)
- o **Q4**: NF/Act: intuitive-feeling (the primary energy fueling inspired *act*ion)

- Your behavior in every moment is a reflection of the ACQ you are engaging. Therefore, awareness of how your behavior maps to the AC supports living in a state of alignment and balance.

  - o You promote *balance* by developing skills that support each of the four ACQs.
  - o You establish *alignment* by learning when the skills of a specific quadrant are needed.

- Your dominant quadrant (DQ) explains your preference for perceiving and judging and provides insight about your strengths and the skills you feel most comfortable employing.

- You must develop all four ACQ skill sets to effectively interact with the world. Enhancing the skills of your less-dominant quadrants (LDQs) strengthens your ability to address diverse circumstances and manage stress.

- The ABCs of Authenticity remind you to choose alignment and balance. By strengthening your commitment to conscious choice, you can learn to manage cycles of success and enhance the quality of your life.

The ultimate source of our happiness
is our mental attitude.
—Dalai Lama

The only person you are destined to
become is the one you decide to be.
—Ralph Waldo Emerson

What we think, we become.
—Buddha

CHAPTER 2
ALIGNMENT

KNOWING HOW TO CREATE ALIGNMENT in your life and relationships is essential to experiencing and sustaining success and harmony. Using your Authenticity Compass helps you identify your strengths and the skill sets that may need development to create alignment in all the situations you face. Once you understand the connection between PDCA (Plan-Do-Check-Act) cycle activities and how to best apply the skill sets of each ACQ, you learn to establish alignment and promote success in each domain of your life.

In this chapter, you will learn how to establish personal and group alignment using your Authenticity Compass. To facilitate this learning, the PDCA Cycle and two supporting alignment principles—systems thinking and active listening—are explored, and an exercise to apply them is provided. Attaining alignment and sustainable success is hindered by many things, and research shows that stress is a dominant one. Therefore, a section is dedicated to stress management that includes an assessment tool called the Present Life Experience Profile (PLEP). This exercise is designed to examine the impact of stress on your well-being in key life domains and provide you with a starting point for specific skill development.

Alignment plays a defining role in human behavior, whether you are considering individuals or groups representing families, communities or global organizations. When you are in alignment, you respond effectively to the people and circumstances that define your life—you experience a positive state of being. In contrast, when you are not in alignment, you experience a negative state of being, such as constant stress from work that may not best suit you or an unaligned relationship's frequent conflict.

Essential Skill Development

You learned in chapter 1 that attaining alignment begins with establishing awareness of your own dominant quadrant (DQ) and your less-dominant quadrants (LDQs). Then, to successfully interact with the diverse individuals and circumstances in your life, you need a variety of cognitive and behavioral skills at your disposal (i.e., those associated with all four Authenticity Compass quadrants, or ACQs). Situations requiring the skills that come most naturally to you (i.e., those of your dominant quadrant) are most likely the easiest for you to engage. However, life is dynamic, so it is vital to your well-being to develop the skills needed to effectively respond to any situation. For example, happy individuals choose to perceive and judge their circumstances, relationships, and interactions in ways that promote their sense of alignment. They have developed skills that enable them to align with each situation they face. In other words, they can readily access the skill sets associated with the appropriate ACQ as needed.

Well-functioning families encourage and support membership alignment. Individuals within these families respect each other's needs and aspirations. Key roles within the home are defined. Responsibilities for tasks such as meal preparation and home upkeep are often shared. There is a committed focus on personal growth. No matter a person's age, it is understood that a happy home requires the ongoing nurturance of one another's peace of mind and physical well-being. In Authenticity Compass terms, ACQ skills are nurtured such that each family member regularly experiences success within his or her respective life domains. Similarly, alignment within groups can be witnessed in the nature of their relationships, the activities they embrace, and the degree of fulfillment they experience. Where there is strong group alignment you will find harmonious cooperation, clear two-way communication, and people engaged in tasks and projects that bring joy to themselves and others. Every member can articulate the group's purpose and objectives as well as each person's specific role—knowledge that strongly supports the agility and sustainability of the group.

The Authenticity Compass

An often described attribute of being in alignment is the invigorating energy you experience. Some characterize this experience as being in flow with the universe. Mihaly Csikszentmihalyi, a Hungarian psychologist who dedicated his career to the study of flow, defines it as "being completely involved in an activity for its own sake and using your skills to the utmost."[1] When you are in flow, you are fully engaged. You are aligned in the moment with the people and/or circumstances you are facing. You are fulfilled. Time flies. There is just being one with your activity.

Alignment and, ideally, flow come naturally when situations call for you to use the skills of your DQ. However, as already explained, you cannot always rely solely on your DQ; life's challenges require you to develop skills that support all four ACQs. This is because circumstances can call for the skills of one of your less-dominant quadrants, but if it is underdeveloped, you are likely to be ineffective and experience a negative state of being, like stress or anxiety. For example, if your DQ is Q1 (NT/Plan) and you become the sole caretaker of your elderly parent, you will only get so far with your logical Q1 DQ skills before you become drained. Your best recourse is to hire a caregiver while you develop your Q3 LDQ skills (SF/Check), which center around people issues and caretaking.

The next section focuses on promoting alignment using cycles of success. First, here is a quick diagnostic test you can use to determine the degree of alignment that currently exists in any group you are a member of and whose performance is important to you. While organizations are the typical audience for exercises like these, it can be both fun and enlightening for families, sports teams, clubs, and so on to get results from this alignment test.

Exercise 4. Group Alignment

Ask each member individually:

1. How would you describe the group's purpose?
2. How would you describe your role in the group?

3. How would you describe the roles of the other members in the group?

Now review the responses and ask yourself:

A. Does everyone have the same understanding of the group's purpose?
B. Does role clarity exist? (i.e., Does each person clearly understand his or her role as well as the specific roles held by the other members of the group?)

If you can answer yes to questions A and B, you have strong alignment. If you cannot, you have work to do.

PDCA Cycles and Systems Thinking to Promote Alignment

The Authenticity Compass encourages alignment within the personal and professional domains of your life. By requiring you to recognize the ACQ skills you are employing in your interactions with others, you become more conscious of your DQ's influence and learn to make use of your LDQs, when needed, to achieve alignment. The PDCA Cycle component of your Authenticity Compass encourages alignment by describing and interrelating the activities of your life in a manner that engages cycles of success.

As discussed previously, Deming's research proved the alignment of the four PDCA activities (represented in the AC) promotes the success of any process. Deming's PDCA framework is rooted in *systems thinking*, a principle that explains how an entire system or set of processes hangs together by describing the linkages and interactions that shape its behavior. Understanding systems thinking is instrumental to sustainable success because you must think holistically about any system to maintain its alignment and balance. For example, if you think of your life as an overarching system governed by a large PDCA Cycle, you can use systems thinking to holistically manage the many smaller PDCA Cycles within it (work, health, finances, etc.) to optimize your well-being. Optimizing your whole self requires identifying and supporting the interdependencies that exist between the domains that define your unique life system, such as the relationship between work (making money) and finances (managing money) or work (managing time spent at your job) and family life (spending quality time with loved ones). You will find a list of major life domains in the PLEP exercise presented at the close of this chapter. This exercise will help you assess how well supported each of your key life domains is currently.

Active listening is a learned communication skill that is essential to the maintenance of every successful personal and professional system. Active listening means listening without judgment or interruption. It involves asking clarifying questions and responding with affirmative body language. Active listening supports the feedback activities of a well-functioning process. (See figure 5.) *Bidirectional feedback* means assessments and corrective action suggestions are shared in two directions (both forward and backward within a PDCA Cycle). For example, a newly married couple who hope to buy their first home prepare to evaluate their finances. After gathering their financial documentation, the wife starts the discussion by focusing on the data that reflects their current spending habits and how they might make changes to save more money. Her spouse agrees and in turn presents additional thoughts on how they can develop a budget to improve their financial standing. By employing active listening and confirming the key points of their discussion, they ensure a clear understanding of the discussion and the next steps to be taken.

In homes and businesses where systems thinking and active listening are commonplace, it is highly likely that the members of these groups are in purpose-driven alignment. This is true no matter whether the group is composed of a handful of individuals (as it is in most households) or hundreds of people (as is true in many business operations). Optimizing a whole organization requires active listening between and within its subsystems and addressing the feedback generated in a timely manner. Deming's work advocates active-listening-supported systems thinking focused on interrelated PDCA Cycles. It dispels the myth that successful business management can be achieved by top-down edicts.

Figure 5. Promotion of Active Listening in Cycles of Success

The promotion of systems thinking and active listening is a challenging aspect of creating and maintaining cycles of success. When people communicate with honesty and actively listen to one another, they promote transparency and harness the power of alignment. In interpersonal relationships, this power translates to harmony, empowerment, and stability. In business, this power translates to operational excellence, organizational resilience, and, ultimately, sustained profitability. I encourage you to explore the power of alignment by identifying the opportunities for systems thinking and active listening in your own life. While the following is a business example, it does a good job of highlighting how these alignment principles are put into practice.

Customer-Employee Alignment: A Case Example

As president of Fidelity Investments' Retail Division (FRIS), Steve Akin instituted a world-class strategy for customer service by focusing his leadership team on the role alignment plays in the creation of effective, profitable, and sustainable business relationships. This strategy produced a consistently healthy profit margin and a multistate call center organization that doubled in size in less than three years. Akin's approach to business process alignment resulted in loyal customers and employees who knew they were being led by an honest, intelligent man—a man who sincerely cared about their success.

Steve Akin left an indelible mark on Fidelity. Decades after his tenure as the president of FRIS, members of his management team still reminisce about what they accomplished, as well as the joy they experienced working for him. Akin galvanized FRIS's mission to provide the best customer experience in the financial-service industry by establishing a work environment in which the following held true:

- Every employee knew the company's mission and the respective responsibilities they had as individuals to achieve it.
- Employees were clear not only about their own unique roles but also about the role every other member of their team was playing.
- Active listening was encouraged; bidirectional feedback was a standard operating practice within and across business processes.
- Duplication of effort, rework, and wasted efforts were actively avoided and promptly eliminated when identified.

When working to actualize cycles of success, it is necessary to ensure as many of the following conditions for alignment are met as possible:

1. Purpose is clearly communicated.
2. Each activity within the process is resourced and managed.
3. Active listening and bidirectional feedback are in place throughout the process, especially where interdependencies exist among activities and there are influences external to the process at work.

Another alignment success factor is developing awareness of the innate differences in time orientation that often exist between activities. As shown in figure 6, the ACQs, energies, activities, and skill sets on the top half of the graphs are future-oriented, whereas those on the bottom are present-focused.

Figure 6. Present versus Future Focus of AC Quadrants

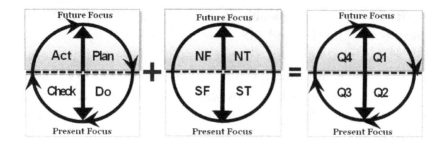

It is essential to recognize the influence time dependency has on the PDCA Cycle. The following outline documents the respective time orientation for each ACQ. The subbullets describe each quadrant's dependency on its adjacent ACQs.

Q1: Planning activities require *future*-oriented intuitive-thinking (NT) skills.

A plan is directed by the vision of what is to be achieved (Q4). The result of planning (Q1) is witnessed in its execution (Q2).

Q2: Execution activities require *present*-state sensing-thinking (ST) skills.

Execution is directed by a plan (Q1). The effectiveness of execution (Q2) is understood through monitoring (Q3).

Q3: Monitoring tasks/caretaking activities require *present*-state sensing-feeling (SF) skills.

Monitoring provides information about what is and what is not working as defined by the plan (Q1). This information drives change management (Q4).

Q4: Change management activities require *future*-oriented intuitive-feeling (NF) skills.

Change management is driven by both the opportunities and the problems identified in monitoring each activity (Q3). The effectiveness of change management (Q4) is witnessed in the plans that result from it (Q1).

By requiring you to recognize the ACQ skills you are employing in your interactions with others, you become more conscious of your DQ's influence and learn to make use of your LDQs (where needed) to achieve alignment. As you review this outline, think about where your DQ fits into the cycle of success. Knowing your area of strength arms you with information about where you shine in the PDCA Cycle. It also provides clues as to why some processes in your life may be more difficult than others, as they may be dependent on skills that are not in your wheelhouse.

The following two stories are real-life examples of PDCA Cycle use. The first story highlights how my DQ is leveraged when I use the PDCA Cycle to manage my family's vacations. The second story demonstrates how the PDCA Cycle helps address destructive tension by creating alignment in a business meeting.

Example 1: Bond Family Vacations

My DQ is Q1. I naturally think ahead and enjoy planning family vacations. My husband's DQ is Q2. He innately focuses on the here and now and enjoys being outside in nature. We both treasure vacationing with our adult children and their growing families.

Here is how we use the PDCA Cycle to ensure we have wonderful vacations.

Plan: I do the planning for each vacation, using information from previous trips, current family input, and data I have gathered from other sources (friends, newspapers, the internet, etc.). Once I find a place that meets our family's varied needs, I seek input from the group. When consensus is achieved, I book the trip. A few weeks before the trip, I check in with everyone to make sure they are all set to go.

Do: Once we arrive at our destination, my husband takes the role of leader, orchestrating the activities. It is natural for him to take responsibility for the execution of the vacation given his dominant quadrant is Q2.

Check: While we are vacationing, I listen to all feedback given to me by my family, especially regarding any snafus that may have occurred. At the close of our time together, we debrief the experience. I review their feedback. We discuss what was liked and disliked and what to avoid and what to repeat in future vacations. I document this information in my vacation journal.

Act: When it is time to plan the next vacation, the current needs and desires of all family members are reviewed. This information along with the knowledge of what worked and what didn't work in prior vacations feeds the planning effort. Our goal is to make sure every vacation is as good as (or better than) the ones we have already had.

Example 2: A Contentious Product-Development Meeting

In software-development companies, meetings to review the needs of the market, release timing, and budgets (as well as numerous additional factors associated with producing a product that customers want) take place between sales people, developers, and other stakeholders.

At the start of this particular meeting, a senior sales manager tells the group he has promised a long-standing, influential customer that a complex feature would be included in the upcoming release. Hearing this, the stunned and angered developers in the room stand up and declare that this feature was not in the agreed-upon user specifications, that several additional weeks of development and testing would be needed, and that the product release would be significantly delayed. The tension in the room becomes palpable as much rides on the on-time product launch, including the developers' bonuses.

As the facilitator of this meeting, I immediately call a fifteen-minute break. When we reconvene, I conduct a level set by reviewing the company's mission statement and confirming the collective commitment of the group to deliver on it. We then agree to respectfully use the PDCA Cycle to discuss the promised feature and its business implications. Here is a high-level summary of the process discussion as it took place:

Plan: Clarify what the influential customer wants. Summarize, at a high level, the technical specifications required to create this feature in the upcoming release. Discuss other customers/markets that may potentially be interested in this feature. Identify the business risks associated with delaying the planned release or not delivering the requested feature to this important customer in this release.

Do: Using input from the cross-functional team present in the meeting, conduct a macrolevel cost/time scenario for what it would take to build, test, and deliver the promised feature. Perform a high-level ROI analysis to quantify risk and benefit.

Check: Review the calculations of cost, time, benefits, and risks that have been presented. Identify, discuss, and evaluate anything that has been left unaccounted for.

Act: Have participants vote on whether to commit to the already agreed-upon release date *or* ask the owners of the company for permission to address the feature in the upcoming release (and, thereby, postpone its launch). The result: Group consensus is reached. The release date will be kept as is. The sales manager will explain to his customer why the new feature will be available in the next release and not in the upcoming one.

Exercise 5. Applying the PDCA Cycle

This exercise asks you to apply the PDCA Cycle framework to a personal or professional situation/process that you want to improve. As you think about your selection, keep in mind that many processes have interrelated subprocesses. So for the purpose of this exercise, if you select a process with subprocesses, only focus at the macrolevel, meaning the most overarching PDCA Cycle. Once you get the hang of this exercise, you are encouraged to apply this methodology to each process and set of subprocesses that you want to improve.

Step 1: At the top of a fresh page in your journal, write down the title of the situation you wish to improve and why you want to improve it. Select something with a clear scope such as eating healthy, improving communication with your boss, or getting more exercise. You may not immediately see this situation as a process, but once you start thinking about the objective, what you are currently doing to achieve it, and what is causing you problems, you will be well on your way to recognizing it as a process. In fact, I hope you will begin to recognize that many of the recurring activities in your life are processes that can be explained and improved by applying PDCA Cycles and systems thinking.

Step 2: Draw the Authenticity Compass in your journal under the situation you just wrote down in step 1, leaving some space to the side. Label the four quadrants using PDCA terminology. (Write "Plan" in Q1, "Do" in Q2, "Check" in Q3, and "Act" in Q4.)

Step 3: List each step of the process in a column beside the Authenticity Compass you just drew. Now, position each listed step into its appropriate ACQ/PDCA step. When you are finished, if there is an ACQ missing an activity, you have found an impediment to success that must be addressed.

Step 4: Rate the current performance of each ACQ using the following color code:

The Authenticity Compass

- Red means needs improvement.
- Yellow means adequate/okay.
- Green means doing well.

Step 5: When there is more than one person involved in a process, it is important to evaluate whether bidirectional feedback and active listening are taking place where needed. The key question to ask is: Does bidirectional feedback exist at each handoff within this process? (Make it a practice to ask this question as you move from one ACQ to the next.)

If yes ... What is the nature of the feedback being given? To whom is it being given? Is this the right person(s) or group(s)? Who else might benefit from the information? Explore whether there are ways to bolster the flow of the feedback by examining the timing, content, packaging, and direction of the information being gathered.

If no ... Identify who needs to listen to whom. Identify what to listen for and how to best optimize information flow.

Step 6: Review the diagram. If applicable, jot down any facts, beliefs, thoughts, or feelings influencing the process that have not yet been documented. Use the same red, yellow, and green color coding (described in step 4) to capture this additional insight about the process. Consider the role that your DQ and LDQs could be playing and journal your thoughts and ideas.

Step 7: Commit to addressing the red areas (i.e., needs improvement). What choices can you make today to positively influence them? These are your action items. Write them down, and commit to following through on each of them by a specific date. Revisit this exercise and its list of action items on the date specified. Determine whether the areas needing improvement have seen positive change. Repeat this PDCA Cycle analysis until you can code all activities yellow (adequate) or green (doing well). Keep in mind that when an activity within a PDCA Cycle is a subprocess, you should consider doing a separate PDCA analysis for it. In these cases, once you have done the required follow-up work, you can return your attention to your macrolevel PDCA assessment.

The Importance of Stress Management

Stress disturbs alignment and hinders well-being. One of the most common triggers of stress occurs when individuals believe the demands of life and work exceed their personal resources.[2] This lack of supply and demand alignment (or its perception) can cause a person to feel overwhelmed and can evoke emotions such as anger, anxiety, depression, and fear. Unfortunately, these emotions can lead to unhealthy choices in diet and lifestyle, which, in turn, can drive people further out of alignment with their world.

The negative effects of stress in your life demand attention and corrective action. To manage stress, you must be aware of its source(s). The Authenticity Compass helps you to identify and address your stressors. Your happiness and success depend upon learning these skills. Exercise 6 is designed to help you identify, by life domain, skills that need development.

Here are six principles of stress management that offer guidance and perspective about one's personal alignment with the world. I learned these principles in the early 1980s while working in the Bio-behavioral Laboratory of the Psychiatry Department at Boston University Medical Center (now Boston Medical Center). They are:

- Stress comes from all areas of your life.
- Stress accumulates.
- What is stressful to one person is not necessarily stressful to another. For example, a wealthy man finds it stressful to pay his bills because he does not like giving away his money. Another man with very little money truly enjoys his bill-paying experiences. They give him a sense of accomplishment and leave him feeling proud of himself.
- Life events such as a job promotion, getting married, having a baby, planning a vacation, or making a big-ticket purchase (such as a home) cause positive stress.

- It is beneficial to your health to decrease as many stressors in your life as possible.
- It is essential to learn *not* to stress about stress.

The nondenominational serenity prayer is actionable advice that can be said during stressful times to gain perspective:

God, grant me the serenity to accept the things I cannot change,
> the strength to change the things I can,
> and the wisdom to know the difference.

This next exercise is designed to build a deeper awareness of your current stressors and the degree to which each contributes to your present life experience (i.e., your alignment with the world and your personal sense of well-being). While the exercise focuses on personal alignment, it can also apply to creating organizational alignment because all employees, including owners and managers, are ultimately responsible for their personal perceptions of and public reactions to their work environments. (Note: Where there is strong employee engagement within a workplace, you tend to find positive stress and exceptional organizational performance.)

Exercise 6. Present Life Experience Profile (PLEP)

This exercise is designed in four parts. The first part asks you to assess your current satisfaction with eight life areas. These domains were selected from stress management research done by Dr. Lyle Miller et al.[3] and from key life areas addressed in financial planning and insurance policy design (e.g., physical health, relationship status, education level, etc.). Completing this exercise generates a Present Life Experience Profile (PLEP) that you will refer to later. Please remember the PLEP is a dynamic assessment. Changes in your circumstances and relationships, as well as your experiences of alignment and balance will alter your profile. As you work with your Authenticity Compass over time, plan to regularly revisit your PLEP.

Exercise 6. (PLEP) Part 1: Assess Key Areas of Your Life

Please think about the following list of areas in your life *right now*.

Rank your satisfaction with each one by placing an X over the most appropriate rating: very satisfied (VS), satisfied (S), dissatisfied (D), or very dissatisfied (VD). Next, write a brief explanation for choosing it. Describe the stress you are experiencing. Feel free to add more areas or to split up existing ones as needed (e.g., rank work life and school life separately). Please be completely honest with yourself, and take as much time as you need. You may prefer to use your journal to conduct this exercise.

Physical Health   VS--------------S---------------D---------------VD

Financial Health   VS--------------S---------------D---------------VD

Emotional Health   VS--------------S---------------D---------------VD
(Do you suffer with anxiety, anger, depression, guilt, fear, or jealousy?)

Close Relationships VS--------------S---------------D---------------VD
(Parents, siblings, spouse, partner, children, coworkers, boss, friends, in-laws, relatives, etc.)

Cognitive Health   VS--------------S---------------D---------------VD
(Do you suffer with poor memory, indecisiveness, confusion, or racing thoughts?)

Leisure Activities/ VS--------------S---------------D---------------VD
Community Involvement
(Evaluate how you spend your time outside of work/school.)

Work/School Life   VS--------------S---------------D---------------VD

Spiritual Life   VS--------------S---------------D---------------VD

The Authenticity Compass

Exercise 6. (PLEP) Part 2: Reflect on Your Stressors

1. Use the results from part 1, and list the areas in rank order in the space provided below. List areas identified as very dissatisfied first, followed by dissatisfied, followed by satisfied. You do not need to list any area with which you are very satisfied. For ease of reference, put the ranking of the life area (i.e., VD, D, or S) in the parentheses provided on the left.
2. Now, thoughtfully respond to each of the following questions for each area you listed. You will most likely need more space than is provided here, so it is recommended that you do this reflection in your journal.
   - What *facts* (people, situations) are presently influencing this area of your life? Where and when are you most affected by these facts/people?
   - What are the *beliefs* you hold about this area of your life? For instance, do you believe you can improve it or that it can never change?
   - What are your *thoughts* about this area of your life? Is it teaching you something? What is it teaching?
   - What are your *feelings* about this area of your life? (Are you upset, angry, frustrated, hurt, sad, resentful, fearful, or hopeless?)

( ) _____

( ) _____

( ) _____

( ) _____

( ) _____

( ) _____

( ) _____

( ) _____

Exercise 6. (PLEP) Part 3: Map Impact of Stress on Your Body/Heart/Mind/Spirit

There is an East Indian proverb that says a person is a house with four rooms: one physical, one mental, one emotional, and one spiritual. Unless we go into every room every day—even if only to keep it aired—we are not a complete person. Many of us tend to live in one room a good deal of the time.

The purpose of this part of the PLEP is to give you a picture of the impact stress may be having on you.

- Review the list you created in part 2. Consider whether each item you listed is presently affecting your physical, emotional, intellectual, or spiritual energy.
- Write that area next to the corresponding square in the following diagram. You can position an area in as many places on the diagram that apply. This means if a particular area (such as your work/school life) is having a negative influence on all four areas of energy, you would place it next to all four squares.
- Now, devote some time to the following questions by writing your responses in your journal: What are your observations about the results? Is there any quadrant without an entry? Are stressors equally distributed all over the diagram or clumped into one area? What does this mean to you? (Validation? A new insight? Actionable Advice?)

Figure 7. Your AC and the Four Rooms

Exercise 6. (PLEP) Part 4: Skill Set Identification

Look at the diagram you just developed in part 3 of this exercise. As you do this, use the following mappings to bolster your awareness:

- Intellectual life maps to mind and intuitive thinking (NT) / planning skills (Q1).
- Physical health maps to body and sensing thinking (ST) / doing skills (Q2).
- Emotional health maps to heart and sensing feeling (SF) / checking skills (Q3).
- Spiritual health maps to soul and intuitive feeling (NF) / inspired action skills (Q4).

Now place an asterisk on your DQ, and answer the following questions in your journal:

- What, if any, stressors are in my dominant quadrant?
- Do the majority of stressors I identified fall in my less-dominant quadrants? If yes, what might this mean?
- Are there more stressors in the quadrant opposite my DQ than any other? If yes, what might this mean?
- What have I learned about myself? Take some time now to identify any short- or long-term changes you would like to make.

Congratulations! By completing all parts of the PLEP Exercise, you have taken steps to raise your awareness and improve your life. You have identified the domains in your life needing the most attention and have spent some time exploring how these areas are influencing your well-being. You now have a reference guide to help you understand the skill sets you may need to develop to experience a greater sense of alignment, well-being, and satisfaction in your life. As you read on, this book will continue to support you on your journey of self-discovery and improvement. Plan to regularly revisit your PLEP. You will be pleasantly surprised by the alignment improvements you can make.

Chapter 2 Takeaways

- Personal alignment is the positive state of being you achieve by responding effectively to the varying circumstances and relationships in your life.

- Alignment comes naturally in situations where you can employ skills of your dominant quadrant (DQ). These tend to be opportunities to experience flow.

- When alignment cannot be achieved using skills of your DQ, you can experience negative stress. This is typically the case when a situation requires less-dominant quadrant (LDQ) skills that are in need of development.

- You maintain alignment by developing all four ACQ skill sets and choosing to employ the ACQ skills that best fit a given situation.

- Applying the PDCA Cycle to any personal or business process encourages alignment by identifying opportunities for improvement.

- The alignment principles of systems thinking such as bidirectional feedback and active listening are essential to PDCA Cycles of success.

- Developing awareness and skills to achieve moment-to-moment alignment is key to your success and happiness and is a primary Authenticity Compass objective. Your PLEP supports the understanding of your alignment challenges on an ongoing basis.

You are the master of your destiny. You can influence, direct and control your own environment. You can make your life what you want it to be.
—Napoleon Hill

If you can't describe what you are doing as a process, you don't know what you are doing.
—W. Edwrds Deming, PhD

CHAPTER 3
BALANCE

MAINTAINING BALANCE IN YOUR LIFE is necessary for sustainable well-being, happiness, and, ultimately, success. By strengthening self-awareness and your conscious choice muscles, your Authenticity Compass encourages your personal growth by preparing you to address the factors responsible for imbalance in your life.

In this chapter, you will learn how to promote your balance and happiness. As in chapter 2, where PDCA Cycles are featured to establish alignment, in this chapter you are shown how to use your PJs to create balance. You are asked to consider factors that may be impeding your experience of personal balance, such as living conditions, thought habits, and limiting beliefs. A mindful meditation exercise supports the clarity and calm needed for introspection. Stories that illustrate how overreliance on one's dominant quadrant (DQ) can cause imbalance conclude with an exercise to further advance your self-awareness.

Personal balance is essential to your happiness and success and, like alignment, is a desired outcome of working with your Authenticity Compass. When you are in balance, you are in a state of mental, physical, emotional, and spiritual equilibrium. You experience well-being because your basic needs are being met and forces are not taxing you. When you can operate from your dominant quadrant, you usually experience a sense of balance because you are perceiving and responding to the world in a manner that feels natural. Maintaining personal balance in your life lays the foundation for sustainable happiness. However, there are so many factors that influence personal balance, from genetic makeup and living conditions to one's personal and professional relationships, it is not surprising that many find sustainable happiness elusive. Yet, despite these factors, research indicates that happiness, to a significant extent, is within your control.[1]

Happiness is subjective—its definition varies from one individual to the next—but *how* you choose to define it can determine whether you will attain it. Many describe happiness as a sense of contentment, pleasure, or joy—a feeling that all is right in my world. Others equate happiness with wealth, even though it has been proven that as long as you are not under financial stress and your basic needs are being met, the more money you have does not make you happier. (In fact, studies show that extra material wealth, beyond a cushion to handle unexpected expenses, bears little or no effect on happiness.[2] Then there are others who rely on relationships or specific events, such as vacations, comedy shows, and goal-oriented achievements for their happiness. When not occupied with these stimuli, they consume their time planning the next activity or reminiscing about events that have already occurred. Unfortunately, their inability to recognize the value of life in the present moment contributes to their feelings of personal imbalance and unhappiness. Seeking happiness outside oneself is unpredictable and unsustainable. Happiness must come from within. Appreciating each moment by learning to be mindful of your perceptions (senses and beliefs), judgments (thoughts and feelings), and behaviors is the most direct path to it.

When psychologist Martin Seligman created the field of positive psychology in the late 1990s, he encouraged his colleagues to study mental wellness with the same focus and commitment they gave to mental illness. The publishing industry witnessed the effect of Seligman's influence. Four thousand books about happiness were published in 2008 as compared to only fifty in 2000. Many relevant themes emanated from this expanding body of literature, including the following three:

- We each play an active role in our experience of happiness.
- Happy people address and eliminate conflict. They know allowing disagreements to linger without resolution detracts from their happiness.

- Positive experiences have a longer-lasting influence on our state of happiness than material possessions do. (For example, having a lunch date with a friend will likely have a more enduring influence on your happiness than spending the same amount of money on a piece of clothing.)

Innovative research done by Sonja Lyubomirsky, PhD, best-selling author of *The How of Happiness: A Scientific Approach to Getting the Life You Want*, furthered happiness research in the field of positive psychology. Her data-driven findings reveal that approximately 40 percent of your happiness is within your control and is based on what you think and do. According to this research, the remaining 60 percent is influenced by your genetics (50 percent) and your circumstances (10 percent). In her book, Lyubomirsky stresses that while you cannot change your genetics and it may be difficult to change your circumstances, by working on changing your behaviors, such as breaking lifelong bad habits and creating positive ones (e.g., focusing on optimism, gratitude, forgiveness, mindfulness, kindness, relationship health, and physical and spiritual wellness), you not only feel better, but you experience better health, higher productivity, and greater resiliency.

Your Authenticity Compass helps you actualize these findings and take charge of your happiness in the following ways:

- Reminding you that your perception influences your judgment and your judgment influences your behavior increases your self-awareness and gives you more control over your life.
- By compelling you to evaluate your perceptions (sensing/facts and intuition/beliefs), judgments (thoughts and feelings), and behaviors in each situation—especially negative ones—you learn to make conscious choices that promote your balance and happiness because how you use your PJs and interact with your world determines your moment-to-moment life experience.
- Identifying and evolving your less-dominant ACQ skill sets that require development equips you to consistently choose the

ACQ that maintains your personal balance as you align with changing life dynamics (instead of defaulting to your DQ).

Strengthening your self-awareness and conscious choice skills is a primary objective of using the Authenticity Compass. It positions you to readily identify and address the factors influencing your personal balance and increases your capacity to maintain mental, physical, emotional, and spiritual equilibrium. The more you use your Authenticity Compass, the easier it will become to create healthy cognitive and behavioral habits that support a happy and balanced way of life.

Understanding Key Factors Influencing Balance

In order to achieve balance and improve your life journey, you must first attend to the factors negatively influencing you. The East Indian proverb presented in the last exercise of chapter 2 encourages self-examination by asking you to think of yourself as a house with four rooms that represent your physical, mental, emotional, and spiritual states of being. By giving balanced attention to these four rooms and addressing the stressors influencing your body, mind, heart, and soul, you promote balance and happiness. The following five areas are presented to help you examine some of the major factors that affect your four rooms.

1. Abraham Maslow: Hierarchy of Needs

If your basic needs are not met, it is unlikely you will achieve personal balance or have the capacity to achieve happiness and success. Abraham Maslow, a psychology professor at Brandeis University from 1951 to 1969 and the founder of the field of humanistic psychology, identified a five-level hierarchy of human needs. His model of how human behavior is motivated is presented in ascending order as follows (see also figure 8):

First: survival (the physiological need for air, food, and water)

Second: security (the need for safety, order, and stability)

Third: love (the need to experience love and belonging)

Fourth: esteem (the need to be competent and recognized as such)

Fifth: self-actualization (the need to live one's purpose)

Maslow referred to the first four levels of his hierarchy as deficit needs because if you do not have enough of any one of them, you can experience stress until that need is fulfilled. For those who live in modern society, it is easy to take basic luxuries such as clean water, food, shelter, and safety for granted, but your personal balance will immediately be compromised if you ever find yourself in a situation where any one or more of these are absent.

At the top of the pyramid (the fifth level) is self-actualization, based on his theory that every person wants to reach his or her full potential. Maslow discovered that people who achieve this level have a clear sense of meaning and purpose in life, accurately perceive reality, and think altruistically about humanity (e.g., Albert Einstein and Henry David Thoreau). A grandfather of the field of positive psychology, Maslow defined self-actualization by studying the positive qualities in people and the times when they felt in harmony with themselves and their environment. He referred to these times as peak experiences, describing them as profound moments of love, understanding, and happiness.

Figure 8. Maslow's Hierarchy of Needs

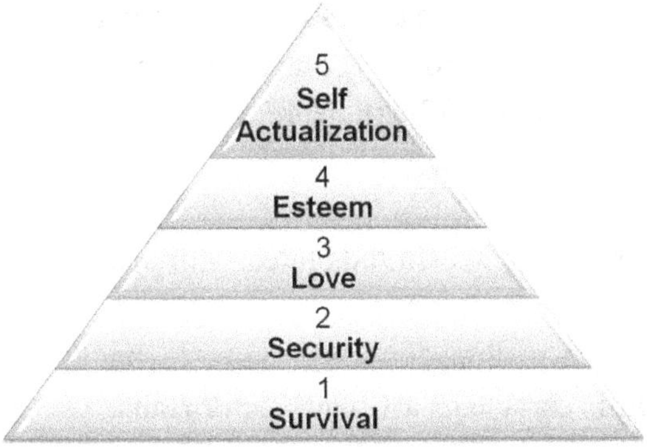

```
        5
       Self
    Actualization
        4
      Esteem
        3
       Love
        2
     Security
        1
     Survival
```

Early in his career, Maslow speculated that each level of need had to be fulfilled before moving to the next, but as his research evolved, he discussed the hierarchy as being relatively fluid because people frequently experience several needs at the same time. As such, by the end of his career, he deduced that self-actualization was not an automatic result of meeting the first four levels of need. Maslow's lifelong study of human potential resulted in his conclusion that sustainable happiness requires commitment to self-awareness. Self-awareness enables self-improvement and supports the occurrence of peak experiences.

The work of both Jung and Deming supports Maslow's research that self-improvement depends upon self-awareness. Jung taught that you cannot achieve personal balance if you do not identify what is causing you to be unbalanced. Deming proved that you cannot align with your circumstances if you do not understand your purpose.

- ☐ Take time now to consider each level of Maslow's Hierarchy of Needs with respect to your life experience. In your journal, write about which needs, if any, have affected your balance in the past and which are affecting your balance today. Do you have deficit needs? Document these in your journal. If you have needs but are not actively working on them, describe what you could be doing to meet them. What insights and action plans do you glean from this?

2. External Forces

External forces influence a person's state of balance. Some of these forces are beyond an individual's control and are associated with what some call the lottery of one's birth. Here is a list of some well recognized forces:

- Birth location (e.g., United States, China, Europe, North Korea, India)
- Current place of residence (e.g., rural, urban, city, town, village)
- Economic class (e.g., affluent, comfortable, poor)

- Religious upbringing (e.g., Jewish, Christian, Islam, Hindu, Buddhist)
- Birth order (e.g., only child, first, second, middle, last)
- Education (highest level achieved: high school, college, professional level, etc.)
- Occupation (Do you have the perfect job? Are you unemployed or underemployed?)
- Living situation (Do you live alone? Is your home peaceful? Do you move often?)
- Health of family members (Are you dealing with the sickness or recent death of a loved one?)

People often attribute unhappiness to their circumstances. However, Sonya Lyubomirsky's finding that only a relatively small percentage of your happiness is attributable to your circumstances should be considered. This means your responses to your circumstances carry more weight in determining your happiness than the circumstances themselves. By recognizing the negative effect certain external forces have on you, you can position yourself to consciously choose a different response—one that promotes as opposed to undermines balance. How external factors influence human potential and resilience is an ongoing area of psychological research.

> ☐ Take a few minutes right now to consider the list above and write in your journal any external factors that affect your daily balance and happiness. These may even be lingering from your childhood. Capturing your feelings, thoughts, and beliefs in writing about these circumstances is a powerful way to elevate your self-awareness and help you put your circumstances in a new perspective.

3. Extroversion versus Introversion

Jung introduced the terms *extroversion* and *introversion* to the field of psychology to explain that people fuel their mental energy either by turning outward or by turning inward. While extroverts get energy from being with others, introverts get replenishing energy from their alone time. Depending on how you naturally fuel your energy, it is easy to see how your personal balance can be affected in certain situations. For example, consider your experiences in business, family, or other group meetings. These settings typically highlight the fact that extroverts tend to dominate group discussions, while introverts tend to be drowned out. This often-witnessed dynamic is especially problematic when introverts have the subject matter expertise, yet extroverts dominate the conversation. If you are a manager, teacher, or a parent, understanding the role self-awareness plays in creating optimum, balanced group participation is essential. You can significantly improve your group's dynamics by mentoring extroverts to appropriately temper their commentary to provide space for introverts to be heard and by mentoring introverts to use their voices when they have value to add.

Jung taught that having proficiency in both extroversion and introversion is essential for everyone, given that the breadth of one's development is gained through extroversion, while its depth occurs through introversion. Recognizing the degree of influence your introversion or extroversion has on your personal balance is essential. This is especially true in times of negative stress.

- ❐ Think about a time when your introversion or extroversion tendencies contributed to your sense of imbalance and stress, and write about it in your journal. Now visualize the same situation with a different response on your part that results in a less stressful outcome, and write about it. Elaborate on the differences in your behavior and PJs from one scenario to the next. What insights can you glean from this?

4. Limiting Beliefs

You may have beliefs that hold you back in life and affect your personal balance on a daily basis. Your core beliefs form the foundation of who you are; many are established early in life without your knowing. This is because as children we naturally assimilate the religious, social, political, and economic beliefs of our families and don't question whether they are right or wrong or if they will best support our balance and alignment later in life. Dissimilar beliefs drive different perceptions between people and are the root cause of most if not all conflict. Ironically, most people do not consciously understand the core beliefs that dictate how they think about themselves and their interactions with others. They have yet to engage with their Authenticity Compass.

It is critical to identify your core beliefs, especially negative ones, because beliefs serve as filters for incoming information (i.e., fact filters) and, as such, determine what you think and feel. For example, if Gwen holds the belief that she is not good enough, she will use information that she receives at home and at work to support it. She may even interpret positive praise, when given, as being obligatory or sarcastic. Believing she is not good enough causes Gwen to live in a chronic state of low self-esteem.

A straightforward technique for uncovering the limiting beliefs that may be serving as the root cause of stress and unhappiness in your life is to ask yourself: Why is this upsetting me? Keep asking why until you identify the belief(s) that are driving your negative thoughts and feelings. Identifying these beliefs is necessary if you wish to replace them with healthier ones—ones that provide greater confidence and happiness and set you up for success (or, at the very least, less stress).

It is also helpful to identify your locus of control because it determines where you believe responsibility lies when you are affected by events in your life. If you have a strong internal locus, you might believe you have control over the events in your life and take credit or blame as appropriate. Conversely, if you have a strong external locus, you are likely to believe the events in your life are beyond your control and blame others when things go awry. Because the reality is usually somewhere in between, you can easily be thrown off balance if you fall into one of these extreme states.

- ❐ Take time now to think about a time of imbalance and stress and consider what belief(s) contributed to your sense of imbalance. Can you identify your locus of control? Write about it in your journal. Now ask yourself why this upset you. Keep asking yourself *why* until you identify the core belief driving your thoughts and feelings. Document this line of questions and answers in your journal. Can you identify the moment this belief was formed or a person it can be attributed to? What insights can you glean from this? Developing this level of self-awareness is what it takes to make positive changes in your beliefs that influence your perceptions, thoughts, feelings, and behaviors.

5. Thought Habits

To achieve and maintain balance, it is essential to free yourself of thought habits that do not serve you. The previous section discussed the importance of identifying the limiting beliefs that feed negative or twisted thinking. Here you are asked to notice the regularity and content of your self-talk. For example, do you tend to take things too personally? Do you constantly compare yourself to others? Do you find yourself regularly envying others? Are you always seeing the glass half empty? Take time now to journal about thought habits that may be negatively impacting you. These are the type of thinking patterns that you need to actively work at correcting because they disturb your personal state of balance. Be advised, however, if you find yourself in the grip of negative thoughts or feelings (such as grief, depression, anger, hatred, envy, greed, etc.) for any prolonged period of time, please seek the assistance of a qualified mental health professional. Your personal balance and well-being requires the resolution of these toxic feelings.

In addition to negative thinking, you may find it difficult to achieve personal balance because of the amount of time you are focused on the past or the future. For example, some people fixate on how a past occurrence defines them (e.g., a death, an accident, or a layoff). This orientation keeps them stuck in the past and puts blinders on their ability to see current opportunities and circumstances for what they are. Others put significant focus on their wants or concerns for the future and, therefore, are also not able to fully appreciate all that is taking place in the moment. Learning to be here now means learning to stay present rather than spending an inordinate amount of time either thinking about the future or mulling over the past.

Being present for some may prove more challenging than it is for others given the role of one's DQ. As was discussed in the previous chapter, those with a DQ in the bottom half of the AC (Q2 and Q3) tend to have an easier time being present-focused than those with a DQ in the top half of the AC (Q1 and Q4).

Regardless of your quadrant dominance, maintaining balance in life requires developing proficiency in the management of:

- your thoughts about the future (Q1)
- your thoughts about the present (Q2)
- your feelings about the present (Q3)
- your feelings about the future (Q4)

In the following quote from *The Four Insights*, a book by Dr. Alberto Villoldo, a psychologist and medical anthropologist, concern is expressed about the deficit of mindfulness in our society:

> We're either always living in the past and wishing things had been different or focusing on the future and wishing we could control it. We're never fully present in the moment. When we live this way, we become the walking dead.[3]

A calm mind supports your personal balance and is necessary to develop proficiency in managing your thought habits. Quieting your mind strengthens awareness of your true self and allows you to rationally assess the factors contributing to imbalance in order to put them into perspective. Mindfulness and meditation techniques can be learned to help monitor and even correct your thoughts so that you can focus on the things that make a positive difference in your life. Consistently practicing these techniques provides the clarity needed to address thoughts that may be sabotaging your happiness and success and understand the immediate steps you can take to encourage alignment and balance in your life.

Exercise 7. Establishing Mindfulness

Mindfulness encourages purposeful awareness of the present. It is essential for establishing and maintaining a state of personal balance. Meditation, prayer, tai chi, yoga, breathing exercises, and physical exercise are practices that support mindfulness. Engaging in these practices on a regular basis develops the focus and self-awareness required to identify and correct the beliefs, thoughts, and behaviors that are not serving you. Three people who have contributed greatly to the mindfulness movement in the west are Thích Nhất Hạnh, Dr. Herbert Benson, and Dr. Jon Kabat-Zinn. I encourage you to consider the guidance found in their work.

The purpose of the following exercise is to give you a starting point for developing your own mindful meditation practice. Please take a few minutes now to conduct this simple exercise.

- Find a comfortable place sitting up or lying down where you will be undisturbed. You may play quiet instrumental music, listen to nature, or have complete silence. Set a timer for five or ten minutes, leaving yourself a few extra minutes at the end for journaling.
- Now, close your eyes and breathe in through your nose to a count of four saying to yourself, "I am absorbing love from the universe." Then, breathe out through your mouth to a count of four saying, "I am releasing fear." Repeat this breathing exercise for your allotted time.
    - If breathing to a count of four does not feel comfortable, adjust the count up or down to find a comfortable rhythm for you. There are also many alternate phrases you can use while inhaling and exhaling, such as breathing in relaxation, white light, happiness, and so on, and releasing stress, pain, sadness, and other negative emotions. Choose a combination that feels comfortable.
- In your journal, capture any insights you glean from your meditative breathing. Did you notice your mind jumping between things you need to do (future) and past events? Our

fast-paced, demanding world can make it a formidable challenge to be calm and present. The more you practice, the easier it will be to dismiss racing thoughts and stay in the moment.
- Decide how often you can commit to the practice of centering yourself using this technique or others. Write this commitment to yourself in your journal and allot time on your calendar. There are several mindfulness and meditation apps available for download on your smart device that can help you incorporate this daily practice. Remember meditation is to be done without judgment or self-criticism. The more time you dedicate to it, the more benefits you will receive.

Balancing Your Dominant Energy: Four Stories

As previously discussed, circumstances, limiting beliefs, thought habits, and many other factors can bring about imbalance in your life. In addition, an overreliance on your dominant quadrant energy can cause instability and perpetuate unhealthy patterns of behavior. Unfortunately, it is typically easier for people around you to recognize your problematic patterns of behavior than it is for you to do so. When you strengthen your self-awareness and work on developing all four ACQ skill sets, you balance the energy of your DQ, live more consciously, and avoid the types of failures brought about by one-way thinking.

The following four stories are presented to demonstrate the results that can come about from the unbalanced reliance on one's dominant quadrant. Pay particular attention to the story that relates to your own DQ. Each story is followed by a reflection that discusses which ACQ skills would help to balance that DQ's energy. Please note, all stories (in this and all subsequent chapters) are based on real people, though some are composites for illustrative purposes. Names have been changed to protect privacy.

Story 1: Q1 Imbalance—The Scholar (Sage) / Dictator

This story reflects the dominant use of Q1 skills, also referred to as intuitive-thinking, planning energy.

This story examines the life journey of a man who devotes himself to teaching others from his acquired wisdom. Dr. Tom is a scholar.

Dr. Tom's sister, a medical doctor, describes Dr. Tom as an intelligent, objective, high-minded seeker of the truth. His colleagues at the university where he works are extremely proud to have him as a member of their faculty. Dr. Tom received his first PhD at MIT and his second, shortly afterward, at Harvard. His intelligence and dedication put him on a fast track of scientific achievement. His colleagues are regularly amazed by the results of his work and his humility. Dr. Tom's sound research and ability to easily explain cognitively complex science have helped position his lab as one of the best academic laboratories in the United States. Dr. Tom and his students are often recognized for advancing the world's knowledge and application of bioengineering. A highly esteemed scientific journal recently published an opinion that Dr. Tom's team has done more than any other biotechnology group to positively influence the future life of the planet.

As Dr. Tom approaches his sixtieth birthday, he is finding it difficult to adjust to the continual advances in communication technology. His students are collaborating with other research centers at a speed that, from Dr. Tom's perspective, is dangerously quick. Dr. Tom is accustomed to having months of time to validate findings. He believes this time is necessary to avoid applying findings that are false and result in expensive (or worse) consequences. Dr. Tom will not accept the fact that time for rigorous validation no longer exists. Instead, he puts in place a strict protocol to govern all external communication from his lab.

The new rules of communication create tension and discord among his students. These students, living in the age of real-time social media and web-based collaboration tools, believe Dr. Tom is incapable of keeping up with the times. They cannot appreciate his point of view about data control, specifically his rule to hold all new findings close to the vest until their validity is confirmed several times over. In reaction to Dr. Tom's new communication protocol, two of his doctoral students ask for an advisor reassignment, and one of his post-docs transfers to another university. The reason they give for their actions is the same. They cannot thrive in Dr. Tom's dogmatic research environment. In a faculty meeting in which these students' decisions were discussed, Dr. Tom thought, for the very first time, that it was time for him to start planning for his retirement.

Story 1: Reflection

In this story, Dr. Tom's planning efforts (Q1 energy) are so controlling they ultimately drive his students away. The need for a more balanced approach, achieved by tapping into the energy of his other ACQs, is evident. In this case, Dr. Tom would have especially benefited from the development of skills associated with the caretaking energy of the Q3 quadrant (which lies directly opposite his dominant quadrant). Learning to check in with the feelings of his students would have helped Dr. Tom address the blind spot he created by his strong reliance on his Q1-based dominant quadrant.

Scholars are often recognized for their planning skills. However, as is true for many people, they can find themselves uncomfortable with and resistant to change. Do you know anyone who behaves in a dictatorial manner similar to Dr. Tom?

Story 2: Q2 Imbalance—The Hero / Cult Leader

This story reflects the dominant use of Q2 skills, also referred to as sensing-thinking, doing energy.

By the time James entered high school, he had the reputation for being a hardworking kid who could be counted on to get the job done. During his high school career, he received recognition for both his intellectual and athletic abilities. His prowess as the school's star quarterback helped earn him an athletic scholarship to college. Unfortunately, in college he did not make the top-tier cut because other athletes were more skilled at this level. This fact did not deter his commitment to his daily exercise schedule or his involvement in his team's practice sessions. However, it did make him think seriously about where he was headed. In his junior year of college, he became fascinated by the workings of Wall Street and decided to become a stock broker after graduation—a path no one else in his family had taken.

Soon after passing his broker licensing exams, he contacted everyone he knew to tell them he was ready to help them with their investments.' Very quickly, he experienced the same kind of accolades and hero status from his investment advice as he had as a high school quarterback. His parents, siblings, relatives, and friends were delighted with the success James was creating. He also enjoyed adoration from his college buddies, especially ones with whom he regularly played golf. Everyone was making money.

James found himself at the turn of the century with new investment products to offer his clients. These products were backed by instruments such as derivatives and collateralized debt obligations (CDOs), instruments that earned large amounts of money quickly. Unfortunately, they lost large amounts of money just as quickly and contributed to the stock market crash of 2008. As it turned out, James's family, friends, and colleagues followed him into a world of financial pain. In this desperate place of lost money, they wondered, *How could this have happened? Why did we blindly follow James's advice?* His brother captured the sentiment of his family with the statement: "We all joined a movement defined by greed, and we made James our leader!"

The next five years were challenging ones for James both professionally and personally. Blame, criticism, and fear defined his relationships at home and at work. However, James did not give up, and by 2013, many of his friends and family members had regained their trust in his ability to provide them sound financial planning advice.

Story 2: Reflection

Heroes put a strong emphasis on achieving quick results. They are disciplined, goal-focused people who value courage, energy, directed purpose, and giving-your-all teamwork. Tending to be highly competitive, productive individuals who thrive on the development of high-performance teams and, in the extreme, heroes can take on cultlike leadership properties. Their weakness comes as a result of their drive to succeed, and this can put them and the individuals on their teams out of balance. They can burn out teams, and sometimes their teams break down because of intense internal competition.

James's dominant quadrant is Q2, or doing energy. At full bore, the expression of his dominant quadrant was imbalanced, and he encouraged others to blindly invest in the stock market even though stocks are never a sure thing and not always the best option for all investors. Had James developed his Q4 skills (motivating others based on their value systems), he would have strengthened his clients' understanding of the risks associated with stock investing. Tapping into the energies of his adjacent ACQs would have also helped him uncover his clients' unique risk tolerances and the specific short- and long-term goals they had for their investments (Q1, planning, and Q3, relationship building).

Story 3: Q3 Imbalance—The Benevolent Leader / Tyrant

This story reflects the dominant use of Q3 skills, also referred to as sensing-feeling, caretaking energy.

Victoria is the only daughter of four children born to a prominent, wealthy family in Chicago. She grew up a daddy's girl who always did her best at school and at basketball, her father's favorite sport, because she knew the pride that her father took in her accomplishments. Victoria always looked forward to sharing her achievements of the day, the discussion her father would facilitate during the family's dinnertime. Victoria's father was a lawyer who, even though he had a demanding work schedule, always made time to impress upon his children the importance of family, loyalty, and pride.

In her senior year, Victoria became the captain of her school's girls' varsity basketball team, and her grades placed her in the top tier of her class, making her college prospects very good and her father extremely proud. Victoria worked hard for these achievements, her motivation and focus being continually fueled by her father's attention and pride in her performance. The basketball players on her team trusted and respected Victoria. Victoria's athletic ability, her dedication to them and their school, and her drive to win made her a strong captain. Watching this team and Victoria's leadership on the court was exhilarating for anyone who enjoyed the game of basketball. The team went undefeated that season and won the state championship title for their school, and Victoria was praised as an unstoppable hero at school and at home, especially by her father.

Fast-forward twenty-five years. Victoria, now a vice president of customer service for a financial service firm in New York City, has a team of eight senior managers reporting to her. Collectively, Victoria and her team are responsible for managing more than five hundred people. Victoria's weekly staff meetings provide the platform for dynamic discussions in which sports analogies are often used to describe industry, market, and organizational behavior. Victoria sometimes finds herself thinking how similar these staff meetings are to the dinner conversations held with her father and brothers around their dining room table in Chicago. Like her father was to her and her brothers, Victoria is highly protective of and loyal to her team. She expects the same from them. This is why she is beginning to have serious reservations about the team's newest member, Daniel.

Daniel, a recently minted MBA from a distinguished business school on the West Coast, is coming across much too confidently for Victoria's liking in staff meetings. For example, Daniel presented a few ideas in today's meeting that were in stark opposition to Victoria's beliefs and experience. The fact that Daniel did not provide Victoria with a heads-up about his thinking before the meeting exacerbates Victoria's frustration. Victoria recognizes that Daniel's behavior forced her to respond in a manner similar to how her father handled the family discussions he wanted stopped. Victoria clearly heard her father's stern voice behind her own when she addressed Daniel and said, "Clearly you have some interesting ideas, Daniel. However, I do not agree with them and do not want you to continue with your line of thinking in this meeting at this time. Perhaps, you and I can revisit these ideas of yours one-on-one in my office. Let's move on to the next agenda item."

Victoria is truly taken aback when her human resources director comes to her later that day to tell her that several of her direct reports had voiced concern to him about the tyrannical approach she had taken with Daniel that morning. After the HR director leaves her office, Victoria sits at her desk, wondering, *How could they say such a thing? Where is their loyalty? Don't they realize I know what is best for them and the company?* Later that year, the executive coach who was brought in to work with Victoria to strengthen her management effectiveness helps her understand the downside of positioning herself as the all-knowing leader.

Story 3: Reflection

We can learn from this story about a benevolent leader who unknowingly became a tyrant. In this case, we see out-of-balance, in-the-moment, caretaking (Q3) energy. If Victoria regularly discussed business strategy with her direct reports during their weekly one-on-one meetings, she could have learned about, and privately discussed, Daniel's ideas. This Q1 management practice could have prevented the public confrontation that took place. By working with the Authenticity Compass and staying mindful of the role each quadrant plays in the Cycle of Success, leaders like Victoria can develop the skills needed to leverage the thoughts and ideas of others.

Do you know someone who absolutely loves being in charge? By this I mean someone who can be counted on to get things done, who loves bringing people together, and who regularly tells others what they should do and when and how they should do it? Growing up, most of us had at least one friend or knew of a classmate or teammate who just had to be the boss. My mother-in-law had an amusing name for this person. It was Mr. or Miss Bossy Boots.

In the workplace, a take-charge attitude is typically respected. People who like to rule appreciate the ability to make things happen. They value orderliness, and they understand power structures. They often establish hierarchies to ensure they have the personal support they need to govern their work environments. (It should also be noted that sometimes established hierarchies can negatively influence a leader's effectiveness because of the attention they require to be maintained.)

Story 4: Q4 Imbalance—The Lover / Con Artist

This story reflects the dominant use of Q4 skills, also referred to as intuitive-feeling, inspirational energy.

Ever since Joanne was a little girl she put much effort into her appearance. In high school, she would not leave home without putting her face on. During this phase of her life, her family frequently complained that she spent too much time in front of a mirror. Like other women in her family, Joanne has strong fashion sense. Her artistic flair is demonstrated by her unique use of accessories, especially jewelry and scarves. She never seems to experience bad hair days, and her hands are always beautifully manicured. Joanne is now a photographer who works out of her Seattle apartment. Visiting her space is like visiting a photo gallery. Her walls are covered with pictures of intriguing people and places and awe-inspiring nature shots. Over the years, Joanne has had several boyfriends. Her closest friends have come to the conclusion that Joanne is not capable of committing to a long-term relationship.

A few years ago, one of Joanne's closest friends, Ann, had a cousin, William, visiting from Germany. When William met Joanne, he was immediately smitten with her beauty, her style, and her dynamic personality. The fact that Joanne was in a committed relationship with someone else did not deter William's pursuit of her attention. It did not come as a surprise to her friends when—within a fairly short amount of time—Joanne broke up with David, the man she had been with for two years, to begin a relationship with William. As this relationship was taking shape, Ann tried her best to explain to her cousin that Joanne was the beautiful, loving woman she presented herself to be but that she was also someone to fear because her loyalty was only to herself. William needed to know the history of men who preceded him. What he saw as a confident, independent, beautiful woman was also a woman with a deep-rooted need to obtain and maintain beauty. If William were to closely examine Joanne's relationship history, he would find that each man she'd dumped was immediately replaced by someone who brought more beauty, luxury, and comfort into her life.

Ann did not want to call Joanne a con artist, the description David had begun using to describe Joanne since she broke up with him. However, the more she thought about Joanne's relationships, she could see how this might be a somewhat fitting description of Joanne's behavior. Ann did not believe that Joanne entered each new relationship with the intent to rob her new lover of all he had to offer. Joanne's breakups occurred because her loyalty was strongly influenced by the physical trappings of life. Ann tried her best to share this con-artist perspective regarding Joanne's behavior with William before he moved to the United States to be with Joanne. However, Ann's words could not outweigh the joy William experienced in his relationship with Joanne. Two years later, Ann found it difficult to keep back the words, "I tried to warn you, William," when Joanne broke up with him to begin a relationship with another man who happened to be a wealthy business executive. The words Ann found to replace, "I told you so," were, "William, I hope you can move through your grief quickly. May the next person you love, love you: your mind, your heart, your body, and your soul … above all material things. Let your relationship with Joanne deepen your understanding of love."

Story 4: Reflection

Lovers are people who value close relationships and a refined quality of life. They tend to create elegant work and living spaces with many amenities. They want the people they spend time with to be close to one another and to make decisions by consensus.

Lovers excel at relationship building, and they put a great deal of effort into making life pleasurable. They tend to demonstrate great passion and devotion not just toward people but to art, music, flowers, jewelry ... anything that positively influences their appearance and the ambiance of their environment.

In keeping with the adage that a person's strength can turn into his or her weakness, lovers frequently get bogged down in emotional dramas and can easily be taken in by flattery. As demonstrated in this story, Joanne allows her dominant quadrant (her Q4 inspirational energy) to drive her behavior in relationships. She sadly lacks the relationship stabilizing skills associated with the other ACQs, such as establishing the mutual goals of a romantic relationship (Q1), being dependable (Q2), and being respectful of others' feelings (Q3). If Joanne were to develop these LDQ skills, she most likely would have fewer relationship breakups.

Key Learning from These Four Stories

The stories you just read demonstrate the types of problems that occur from lack of personal balance and self-awareness. It is easy for people to get so caught up in the power of their DQ that they become blind to the effect their behavior is having on their own happiness as well as the happiness of others. The Authenticity Compass reminds you to maintain awareness of your PJs, especially your DQ. Learning to balance the energy of your dominant quadrant with skills associated with your less-dominant quadrants is an effective way to avoid the imbalance that results from DQ overreliance. Identifying patterns of behavior in your life helps you understand the influence of your DQ. By developing all four ACQ skill sets and learning to choose the most appropriate ACQ in each situation you face, you strengthen your ability to align with the world while promoting personal balance in your life.

Exercise 8. Spotting DQ Imbalance

Please take a moment to think about the stories just presented as they relate to your own life. Here are a few questions to stimulate your thinking and journal writing.

- Are there any similar themes between your life and any of the stories? (You may also find it helpful to review the stressors you identified in chapter 2's PLEP assessment.)
- Think about your DQ and recall a challenging experience you have had or are having. Now look again at the story that highlights your DQ. Do you see any commonalities now?
- Now, for the challenging experiences you just identified, is there one or more ACQs that could be useful in balancing your DQ? Which ACQ(s) and specific skills? Document your thoughts in your journal.
- Next, brainstorm some ways to acquire these skills, and write them down. Are there people in your life who are proficient in these skills and whom you can learn from? Classes you can take? Videos you can watch? Put a plan in place for developing skills to balance out your DQ.
- Do you see any of the story themes playing out in the lives of anyone you know? Which stories? Why?

Your dominant quadrant provides an important reference point for understanding your behavior, but it does not explain your behavior in absolute terms. Knowing your DQ positions you to assess whether your go-to DQ skills or the skills of another Authenticity Compass quadrant will best address the circumstances you face. How well you thrive reflects how well you have developed the skills of all four AC quadrants, as well as the conscious choice muscles you need to employ them. As you work with your AC, you will become more skilled at recognizing the DQ characteristics of those around you, your self-awareness will strengthen, and you will be well on your way to living a life with greater personal balance.

Chapter 3 Takeaways

- Promoting personal balance begins with awareness of how you view (perceive), assess (judge), and subsequently behave (apply ACQ skill sets) in your life.

- Only you are accountable for your state of mental, physical, emotional, and spiritual equilibrium and can correct the factors that impede it, such as: limiting beliefs, negative thinking, unwanted patterns of behavior, and problematic overreliance on your dominant quadrant (DQ) energy.

- Imbalance in life often means that you need to adjust your perceptions (beliefs and sensing of facts) and your judgments (thoughts and feelings) by developing skills that support your less-dominant quadrants (LDQs).

- Mindfulness practices strengthen the self-awareness you need to develop all four ACQ skill sets. Learning to be present is essential for you to experience sustainable alignment and balance in life.

Happiness is when what you think, what you say, and what you do are in harmony.
—Mahatma Gandhi

No person, no place, and no thing has any power over us, for "we" are the only thinkers in our mind. When we create peace and harmony and balance in our minds, we will find it in our lives.
—Louise L. Hay

CHAPTER 4
CHOICE

EVERY CHOICE YOU MAKE INFLUENCES your state of alignment and balance. When you live mindfully, you discourage behavior patterns that contribute to an unsatisfying and unhealthy life. By strengthening your self-awareness, you increase your ability to choose healthy behaviors that support your purpose and well-being. By determining the cause-and-effect relationship that exists between your perceptions (sensing of facts and beliefs), your judgments (thoughts and feelings), and your behavior, your Authenticity Compass guides you to make mindful choices that promote your personal balance and alignment with the world. Consciously choosing beneficial behavior patterns establishes your best possible self and your best possible life.

In this chapter, you will learn how to make mindful choices to live an aligned and balanced life. The material examines how core beliefs relate to choices and behavior patterns. You are asked to consider your own life patterns and to identify your present opportunities for positive change. As part of this self-examination, you will complete a two-part legacy exercise that provides insight into a) the gaps between who you are today compared to who you want to be and b) the actions you can take today to close these gaps, ensure you have no regrets, and leave the best legacy you can. Creating the life story you want requires embracing the ABCs of Authenticity—knowing that you have the power to Choose Alignment and Balance and that only you are in control of your life story and happiness. The chapter concludes with three exercises that build upon each other to strengthen your mental function and behavioral self-awareness and reinforce your power of conscious choice. They are:

1. The SNTF Analysis: Enhance your mental function awareness during impactful and/or stressful situations by examining your facts, beliefs, thoughts, and feelings.
2. The SEE Method: Increase behavioral awareness in situations to better understand the influence of your SNTFs on your behavior and the repercussions of the words and actions you choose to employ.
3. Putting Positive Change in Motion: Take steps toward the life you desire by applying mental and behavioral awareness, using ACQ toggling, and engaging PDCA Cycles of success.

Choice is your most important power in life. The choices you make each moment of every day—your choice of words, actions (or lack thereof), thoughts, and feelings, down to the core beliefs you choose to hold—shape every aspect of your life. Yet, the power and precious gift of choice sometimes gets lost in our everyday, modern lives. We multitask, overschedule, rely on smart devices, and frequently lock into routines that have us functioning on autopilot. Because of this, we tend to overlook the things that really matter and, as a result, make choices that do not support our optimal direction in life. Sometimes, these unmindful choices become a way of life and develop into long-standing, problematic patterns of behavior that negatively affect our health, our relationships, and our happiness.

Overworking, lack of self-care, negative self-talk, constant screen time, overeating, overspending, and drinking to excess are common undesired behavior patterns individuals adopt in unmindful states. If these patterns persist over long periods of time, they can spiral out of control before we realize the repercussions of our actions. In our relationships, these negative behavior patterns can show up as habitual blame, shaming, criticism, guilt, codependency, avoidance, dominance, and jealousy.

Many people, even those considered to be the most intelligent and responsible, can go through life perpetuating problematic behaviors that result in their dissatisfaction with themselves and their relationships.

Staying in the behavior seems easier than doing the work to fix it, even though the individual or couple knows on some level that to perpetuate it can, and likely will, have negative, maybe even devastating, consequences. Often fear-based, irrational beliefs such as, "Changing will be more painful than the consequences of staying in this pattern," and "I should get what I want," maintain these problematic behaviors. As a result, individuals and couples (as well as groups, organizations, and governments) get stuck in self-defeating patterns of behavior until they hit a breaking point.

By choosing not to address destructive beliefs, thoughts, feelings, and behavior patterns proactively, we end up maintaining negative states of being that stress our minds, bodies, hearts, and souls. In fact, research shows that prolonged exposure to stressors causes health problems because it keeps our bodies activating an inborn survival mechanism: the fight-or-flight response also referred to as the stress response.[1] This physiological driver of human behavior enabled our ancestors to react to life-threatening situations by triggering a series of chemical and physio-biological reactions in the body. However, our bodies and the world have evolved. We are not fleeing for our lives on a daily basis. Yet, financial pressures, regular arguments with a spouse, sibling, or coworker, or another frequent negative dynamic, can cause the stress response to continually activate.

When this goes on for weeks, months, years, or even decades, we usually end up sick—physically, mentally, and emotionally—and filled with regret. It is unfortunate that it is usually not until these negative behavior patterns affect our health or we are on the brink of disaster with our relationships that we decide it's time to consider a new perspective and a different set of choices. Luckily, every day presents a new opportunity for us to change our lives for the better. We can start today by using the guidance of our Authenticity Compasses to address our problematic behavior patterns and thereby change the course of our lives for the better.

It is important to understand that the family and circumstances you are born into provide the environment within which your fundamental beliefs are established and your personality develops. By the time you are twenty-five years old, the way you prefer to perceive and judge the world is well defined.[2] This is why as you mature, it is critical to closely examine your priorities, understand the perceptions and judgments driving them, and make a habit of consciously choosing the behaviors that promote your alignment and balance. Only you know if the choices you make on a daily basis support your life's purpose, maintain your personal balance, and promote alignment with the people and circumstances defining your life.

Caroline Myss runs workshops and gives lectures all over the world to help people understand how their beliefs, choices, and behavior patterns influence their happiness and lives. In her *New York Times* best-selling book *Sacred Contracts*,[3] she explains how each of us has unconscious beliefs and attitudes (referred to as archetypes) that influence our lives and relationships in both positive and negative ways. On one hand, our archetypes can protect us (the "light" side), but on the other hand, they can undermine our happiness and success (the "shadow" side). For example, we each have a child archetype. Characteristics of the child archetype's light side are being playful and lighthearted, while descriptors of its shadow side are being dependent and irresponsible.

While examining your beliefs, thoughts, feelings, and behaviors, you glean powerful insight when you recognize your repeating patterns (archetypes). Your life is continually defined by the choices you make. Even though factors beyond your control play a role in shaping your circumstances, how you choose to perceive and respond to them is within your control and ultimately defines your life experience.[4] Some helpful questions you can regularly ask yourself are:

- What are my motivations for doing this?
- Am I doing this because it's what I really want, or is there another reason?
- Will doing this ultimately support my balance, put me in alignment, and serve a higher purpose?

Your answers to these questions may encourage you and cause you to make different choices that better serve you.

Choosing Alignment and Balance: Four Examples

The more you apply the ABCs of Authenticity, the more you gain control over every aspect of your life. You choose alignment and balance by developing all four ACQ skill sets and by identifying and eliminating the behaviors that no longer serve you. By understanding how you view and respond to your world by recognizing the facts, beliefs, thoughts, and feelings driving your behavior, you increase your self-awareness and maintain command over your life.

Being mindful of how you react in times of stress provides important information about how well you are applying your ABCs and where you need to focus your energy. The following four stories are provided to reinforce these lessons.

1. Making Decisions Together

Diane, a former CPA turned stay-at-home mom, received a call from her old boss who lost his senior accountant just before the hectic tax season. He explained he needed someone who could hit the ground running, and Diane was the only person he could think of to fill this important position.

Diane had managed the finances in her home for as long as she can remember but had developed anxiety as her family's savings account had steadily declined since she left her job. As their two children grew, so too had the household bills and her stress over money. She didn't share her worries with her hard-working husband so as not to make him feel like he wasn't doing a good job. However, both kids now needed braces, and the house needed many repairs, some major. Leo, her husband, worked long hours, but neither his raise nor the Christmas bonus they were counting on came through. So when the phone call came in from her former employer, Diane accepted the job on the spot. When Leo returned home from work that day, Diane excitedly told him the news about her new job. Instead of the enthusiastic response she expected, Leo became angry about what he described as her "unilateral decision-making." Leo's reaction clearly indicated that he and Diane were not in alignment about her decision to return to work.

Choice viewpoint: When a member of a family or other close-knit group has an important decision to make, it is vital to stop and take the time needed to consider the impact of the decision on the entire system. Gain consensus before moving forward. This is the best way to ensure alignment and balance of the system and its individual members. In this example, when Diane chooses to go back to work, her husband is concerned the resulting changes will cause disruption and stress for everyone in the household. Diane's fear concerning the state of the family's finances drove her to accept the job. Leo is not aware of how worried Diane has been about their financial situation. Therefore, his perceptions and judgments are not aligned with hers. It is in the couple's best interest to discuss the facts and their beliefs, thoughts, and feelings about how Diane returning to work will affect each member of the family and the family unit as a whole prior to any decision being made.

For people in committed relationships to mature as individuals, achieve personal life balance, and experience relationship alignment, open and honest dialogue supported by active listening is essential. Unfortunately, families, teams, and entire organizations often choose to continually ignore these important joint-decision-making principles and find that over time they have members who feel slighted and resentful. In worst-case situations, they sabotage the system in some way. Stable, harmonious relationships within any type of system do not happen by accident. They depend upon respect and conscious, well-articulated, mutually agreed-upon choices. Optimally functioning couples (and groups) take into consideration each individual's perceptions and judgments (i.e., facts, beliefs, thoughts, and feelings) in order to make the best decision for everyone involved.

2. Getting Unstuck

Alex hit the snooze alarm and mumbled to himself, "I don't want to go into the office." Five minutes later, the shriek of the alarm rang again. Alex slammed the buzzer this time, swung his legs out of the bed, and held his face in his hands. "What am I going to do about this job?!" Alex felt hopeless. He watched the news. He knew jobs were scarce. He knew his resume wasn't eye-popping, having worked at the same company for the past twelve years. It also didn't help his anxiety to have witnessed a coworker get walked out the door after the company learned he was seeking a position with a competing firm. "Why can't I just be happy that I have a good-paying job?," he asked himself. Alex quickly showered, dressed, and made his way to work, moving away from the conversation he was having with himself and getting lost in the mechanics of another stressful workday.

Choice viewpoint: When stuck in an undesirable situation, it is time to examine the perceptions and judgments driving our behavior. This is because the perceptions and judgments behind our choices determine our attitude toward and experience of life. If we are not mindful of these choices, they can drive us out of alignment and balance and keep us stuck in unhealthy patterns of behavior.

In this case, by staying in this job, Alex perpetuates unhappiness and imbalance in his life. Alex does not have a strong sense of directed purpose and is not aligned with his position. As a result, the company he works for does not have a motivated, engaged employee. At this crossroad, Alex must reevaluate his facts, beliefs, thoughts, and feelings about his career goals in order to choose to become reengaged in his current position or motivated to move on to a different job that brings him more joy. By enduring job dissatisfaction day after day, month after month for a paycheck, it is important that Alex realizes he is making a choice based on the limiting belief he won't find another job with equal or better compensation.

Unfortunately, all too often, employees choose to stay unhappy in unfulfilling, stressful positions because they share Alex's pessimism about finding a more fulfilling position. Negative, preconceived notions about skills, pay, personnel, reputation, commute, and so on can be reinforced by circumstantial evidence, such as in Alex's case, the coworker being walked off the job. This makes beliefs about how hard change is even stronger. Just as the frog who dies because he does not jump out of the pot of slowly heating water, an employee stuck in this unfulfilling pattern becomes progressively less aligned and engaged with his position, less valuable to his company, and less satisfied with his life. The result is a lose-lose scenario for both the employee and his employer.

By digging into the facts, beliefs, thoughts, and feelings that drive your choices, especially the patterns of behavior that keep you in a negative state of being, you can address the root causes of why you are stuck. The more you hone in on the things that give you purpose in life, the more you restore your sense of balance and alignment with the world. Spending time quieting your thoughts each day helps you ensure your perceptions match the reality of your situation. It also helps you identify the choices, sometimes life-changing, that will translate to job and life satisfaction.

3. Speaking Your Truth

Bill and Ann met in college and were inseparable from the start. Their relationship was playful, affectionate, and carefree. They married after graduation, and Bill was offered a high-powered, dream job that demanded quite a bit of travel. At first, this was exciting for the couple, as Ann spent her days connecting with friends and shopping at high-end boutiques. But soon she realized that Bill's successful career overshadowed their relationship. She stopped caring about the luxuries and longed for the simple days she had with Bill before his big job.

One Thursday morning Ann was in their driveway overseeing two men carrying furniture from their house onto a moving van. Bill, home early from a conference, was pacing back and forth, shaking his head, wringing his hands, and crying. Someone heard Ann say to Bill as she climbed into her Mercedes, "Your career is more important than our relationship. I can't live like this anymore!" Ann screeched away in her Mercedes, leaving Bill in the middle of the road, feeling desperate and alone. Apparently, Bill was not tuned in to the extreme negative effect his travel-intensive job was having on his wife. Their marriage had reached a breaking point because of the poor alignment of their respective needs.

Choice viewpoint: It is not straightforward or easy to balance one's own personal aspirations while simultaneously maintaining alignment with the wants and needs of one's partner. Nor is it always easy to be completely honest with yourself and others about the beliefs, thoughts, and feelings that drive your behaviors. In this story, neither Ann nor Bill exercised clear and open communication or the relationship caretaking required to support a successful marriage. Ann chose not to share with Bill her dissatisfaction concerning the travel demands of his job. Ann's behavior was a reflection of her belief that Bill traveled so much because he didn't love her the way he had in the past. She had been suffering in silence and was now consequently out of balance. Bill chose to ignore or avoid opportunities to check in with Ann regarding the impact his continual absence was having on her. He believed that if he talked to Ann about his feelings, she would perceive him as a weak man, which was the opposite of the image he wanted her to have of him. He thought that by working so hard he was showing his love by giving her all the luxuries she could ever want. Rather than conducting any form of honest communication, trusting that they would listen to each other with an open heart and mind, their unchecked perceptions and judgments ultimately broke down the alignment of their relationship.

In order for any relationship system to flourish, whether it be a marriage, partnership, friendship, or collective, each member must be willing to examine his or her perceptions and judgments (i.e., facts, beliefs, thoughts, and feelings) to access their personal truth and then trust that truth with his or her companion(s). This approach is necessary to determine whether your perceptions match others. (You should never assume!) The ABCs of Authenticity are achieved by listening to your own internal voice, by consistently (and tactfully) maintaining honest dialogue (always employing active listening), and by making decisions jointly. Rewarding, committed relationships are based on truth and trust. People in them consciously choose to nurture both their own balance and that of their partners by using all opportunities to stay in alignment.

4. Seeking First to Understand

Jack, a newly hired vice president from out of state, arrived with a glowing reputation for increasing profitability and improving customer satisfaction. Before arriving, he did considerable online research and critical thinking about his new employer and developed ideas for the strategic plan he wanted to put in place. He, an open-minded visionary, had no idea that the members of his new management team were fierce competitors who each held resentment about not being selected for the vice president position. After all, they considered themselves better candidates than Jack, having direct knowledge of the company's operations, personnel, culture, and, most importantly, its barriers to success.

Fast-forward several months. Jack, now not so new in his role as vice president, left his staff meeting convinced he had facilitated strategic agreement regarding the next steps needed to bolster the company's performance. His direct reports leave the same meeting frustrated by what they perceive as a flawed plan and weak, idealistic leadership. Instead of buying into Jack's vision, his direct reports become more committed to becoming winning individual contributors. When the end-of-year sales reports are released, the results are abysmal. The company's stock price dropped several more points. The board of directors is disappointed and decides to make cutbacks.

Jack's management team is shocked to learn there is a mandated 20 percent reduction in staff across the company, and Jack will be let go. The day after the layoffs, the remaining managers discuss the genuine regret they feel about the outcome. Had they worked better as a team instead of competing with each other and undermining Jack, they likely could have improved the company's performance and preserved the jobs of the staff that were let go.

Choice viewpoint: To succeed in any type of relationship, group, or organization, one must first choose to understand its many facets, especially those that must be experienced, such as its culture. If Jack had chosen to make an effort to better understand the team's well-established competitive culture, he would have realized he had to work on building organizational alignment. Through one-on-one relationship building and the acknowledgment of each manager's perceptions, judgments, and personal goals, Jack might have built understanding and trust over time, resolved lingering resentments, and broken down the competition that existed within the team. By taking the time to first understand, Jack would have realized the serious need that existed to strengthen the team's alignment. Honest consensus among his managers was essential for him to achieve optimum business results. Jack could have initiated alignment by asking the members of his team to share their facts, beliefs, thoughts, and feelings about his proposed plan in a team meeting. With truthful participation, conflicts that needed to be addressed might have been identified. Their resolution most likely would have set Jack, his team, and the company up for success.

Jack's managers also played a destructive role in the outcome of this story. They chose to stay locked in a pattern of competitive behavior, preventing team alignment and obstructing Jack's, the team's, and, ultimately, the organization's success. Team alignment would have been far more likely if Jack's direct reports chose to provide honest input, positioning Jack's strategic plan for success rather than failure.

Four Examples: Reflection

The four stories you have just read illustrate how an individual's choices influence his or her happiness and success and how easy it is to lock into a pattern of behavior that prevents positive outcomes. If any part of these stories resonates with you, it is likely there is opportunity for you to strengthen your ABCs of Authenticity. If you are not satisfied with your own story because you know you are not living your best possible life, you can choose to make changes.

When we adopt patterns of behavior that keep us in a negative state of being (stress, fear, anxiety), we can behave irrationally and lead with a shadow aspect of ourselves as a matter of survival. We then behave in ways that can throw us further out of alignment with our world and create greater imbalance. Taking the time to understand the facts, beliefs, thoughts, and feelings behind our behaviors is the key to making positive changes.

From this point forward, you can consciously choose to align with your circumstances and support your inner state of balance. With the guidance of your Authenticity Compass, you can examine the relationships and patterns of behavior you have developed over time, determine which do not contribute to your alignment and balance, and take corrective action.

- ☐ Take time now to identify *patterns of behavior* in your life. Use a blank page in your journal, and document the patterns of behavior (PoBs) that you can readily identify by sorting them into those that are good and those that are not good (i.e., those that contribute to your alignment and balance and those that do not). Do this by creating two list headers: My Healthy PoBs and the PoBs I want to change. Use a separate page to delve into the facts, beliefs, thoughts, and feelings associated with each behavior you wish to change, and identify actions you can take to make these changes (and by when). Continue to journal about your progress daily or more frequently if possible. Shining a light on your behavior by journaling about it creates awareness that enables you to modify problematic behaviors and strengthen healthy ones.

The more familiar you become with identifying the patterns of behavior that are alive and well in your life, the more you will also begin to recognize behavior patterns that are present in the lives of the people around you. Make a habit of writing about them in your journal. There are many. Only you can be responsible for your behavior patterns. Raising your awareness of how you choose to perceive and respond increases your power of conscious choice. How you choose to respond to the world, no matter what it serves up to you, is completely within your control and is what defines your life experience.

The next section is intended to put the power of choice into perspective and provide advice for living every day to its fullest.

Learning to Live Without Regret

You should not have to receive a life-threatening diagnosis such as cancer to take a hard look at the choices you have made or are making in life. However, we can learn valuable lessons from those who have done so and survived.

Some individuals who face challenging health circumstances often come to understand, maybe for the first time, that they are out of balance and choose to commit to regular exercise, good nutrition, and a spiritual path for strength. Others may realize they are out of alignment with family and friends and commit to strengthening their relationships. These types of realizations explain why it is common to find adult cancer patients reexamining their personal values. For instance, love of material acquisition and wealth accumulation often wane, and commitment to physical health, personal relationships, and community tend to grow. Living mindfully in each moment with unconditional love and respect for all living things becomes of utmost importance. Valerie Harper, an actress known for her role as Rhoda Morgenstern in a popular 1970s television series called the *Mary Tyler Moore Show*, put choice into profound perspective in a 2013 interview on ABC News's *Good Morning America*. Valerie (fighting inoperable brain cancer) said that we need to accept the fact that we are all terminal (eventually). We should not wait for a life-threatening diagnosis to choose to live our lives to the fullest!

I can personally attest to the tenet "cancer taught me how to live." Statements such as this are said in treatment centers across this country. The explanation is simple and well documented in research on death and dying.[5] After the shock, anger, and resentment of a potentially terminal diagnosis passes and patients accept time on earth is finite, they tend to make choices in a more conscious manner than ever before. This was true for me. Cancer forced me to think about the meaning of life. I turned to the writings of philosophers, psychologists, and religious scholars for guidance and learned a person must look within herself for direction. I had to make choices about how to change my perspective and life so I could live my best life possible. Here is a summary of where I am on my journey today:

- I live consciously. I accept my physical limitations and remain dedicated to the activities that support their improvement. I am grateful for my life energy.
- I love my family, friends, colleagues, and caregivers unconditionally.
- I apply my good days to the study of authenticity and the caretaking of my physical, emotional, intellectual, and spiritual well-being.
- I help others when I am able by mentoring in my areas of knowledge and expertise.

The helpful directives, strength, and comfort I sought during the dark days of my health journey came from many sources, including Eckhart Tolle's books, *The Power of Now*[6] and *A New Earth: Awakening to Your Life's Purpose*;[7] Viktor Frankl's book, *Man's Search for Meaning*,[8] and Don Ruiz's book, *The Four Agreements: A Practical Guide to Personal Freedom*.[9] I hope you can also benefit from the collective wisdom these sources provide. May they guide you (as they did me) to live your life fully, happily, and successfully every day.

It is well documented that people die in states of regret because of the choices they made.[10] My own battle with cancer and living with rheumatoid arthritis has heightened my awareness of the role choice plays in life. For instance, choices about how to and with whom we spend our limited time and energy is critical. When made consciously, these decisions can be quite challenging at times because they force us to be brutally honest with ourselves about our circumstances and our relationships. To live without regret requires continually making the best choice in the moment. Choices that effectively address (align with) the external forces you face and permit you to maintain a sense of personal balance lead you to the best life possible.

One way to ensure you are on the right path is to conduct a legacy exercise. This is done by examining the legacy you are currently creating and comparing it to the one you wish to leave. Doing this exercise generates insights about behaviors in your life you would like to strengthen, modify, or eliminate; plans you wish to execute; and connections you want to make. You can choose the legacy you want to leave. This exercise will reveal whether you are on track.

Exercise 9. Your Legacy

Part A: Your Obituary

The impact you have on the world is determined by the choices you make over your lifetime. Writing your own obituary is an illuminating exercise (and for some, maybe a little bit scary). Its purpose is to help you develop awareness of the legacy you are creating. For example: What would others say about your life if you were to die today? What lasting impressions are you leaving? Would others say you have a purpose? What is it? Do you have a passion for something? Are you raising a family? Are you an active member of an organization? How would you describe your relationships at home and at work? Is your legacy one of loving-kindness? Is your legacy one of learning because you are teaching something that will be appreciated long after your death?

Step 1. *Reflect*: Spend a few moments in quiet reflection to think about these questions and the legacy you are currently creating.

Step 2. *Write your obituary*: Now, turn to your journal, and write your obituary (leaving out the place and date of death, of course). Focus on your relationships, schooling, career, accomplishments, travel, hobbies, and activities with friends, community, and others.

Step 3. *Create a plan*: After you have written your obituary, you may feel compelled to create a list of action items you want to address, goals you want to achieve, relationships you want to build, and so on. Journal your list of action items now. Consider each area of your life as you create this list. (You can use the eight PLEP areas from chapter 2 for guidance.) Make notes next to each item, being specific about what, when, and how to accomplish each one. This exercise will help you establish a plan to make the legacy you wish to create a reality.

Part B: Your Regrets

It is not uncommon to feel some regret after doing the obituary exercise. Identifying regrets is helpful because they can key you into problematic patterns of behavior. Here are a few examples: Do you regret not doing a better job at planning for retirement, executing plans to build a business, taking better physical care of yourself, motivating your children, or, perhaps, just taking a yearly vacation?

Step 1. *List your regrets:* Take as much time as you need to specifically articulate any regrets you have at this moment. Again, consider each domain of your life (e.g., family, community, personal health, financial health, etc.). Write them down in your journal. For each regret you identify, write down any facts, beliefs, thoughts, or feelings that come to mind.

If you have a regret, your inner voice is crying for attention (alignment and balance!). You may find your regret maps to the energy of a less-dominant Authenticity Compass quadrant. It is highly likely that it does.

Step 2. *Map your regrets to the AC:* Explain your regret(s) in terms of how you are perceiving and judging by identifying the ACQ(s) it belongs to (Q1, Q2, Q3, and/or Q4). Here are ACQ-specific questions to help you categorize your regrets:

- (Q1) Not planning something that is important to you? (retirement, vacation)
- (Q2) Not doing something you wish you had? (starting a business) Doing or saying something you wish you hadn't?
- (Q3) Not taking care of someone or yourself? (exercise, meditation)
- (Q4) Not being inspired or able to motivate yourself or another? (mentoring your employees, students, or children)

Step 3. *Use regrets to identify skill development needs:* Consider how the regrets you identified map to your ACQs. Document any skills you may need to develop to address these regrets.

Step 4. *Plan your attack:* For each regret you identified, create a specific plan of action to address it, providing as many details as possible, such as: decisions you need to make, specific skills you need to acquire, constraints you must address, relationships you need to build, and so forth. When can you start executing your plan? Be brutally honest with yourself. Consider how this plan relates to your desired Legacy (from part A of this exercise).

Step 5. *Leverage the PDCA Cycle of Success:* Once you have a Plan to address your regrets, begin prioritizing and executing the tasks (Do). Keep tabs on yourself in your journal to track how well you are doing against your plan (Check). As you progress, make any needed adjustments that help you stay focused on alignment and balance (Act). Most importantly, keep trying, and don't judge yourself.

Please take comfort in knowing that as long as you are alive, you have options. It is not too late to address your regrets and create the legacy you want.

Creating Your Best Life: Awareness and Action

You create your own life story. To be true to yourself and others and live a life that allows you to embrace your purpose and passion, you must strengthen your self-awareness and act on your insights. This begins by paying attention to how you perceive and judge your life. Every fact, belief, thought, and feeling you experience results in a response. Your responses string together over the course of your life to create your life's narrative. Once you understand that your perceptions and judgments are the drivers of your behavior, you become empowered to choose your responses and, ultimately, create your best possible life. Developing this level of self-knowledge not only supports your ability to create the rewarding life you deserve but also provides you with the insights you need to make choices that maintain harmony in your relationships.

The remainder of this chapter provides exercises that build upon each other to create a platform for positive change. The first of the three focuses on the mental-function building blocks that drive behavior: the sensing (facts) and intuition (beliefs) that make up your perceptions and the thoughts and feelings that make up your judgments. It is helpful to keep in mind as you do this exercise that your perceptions and judgments always work as PJ pairs.

Exercise 10. The SNTF Analysis: Increasing Self-Awareness

This SNTF exercise utilizes a self-questioning technique to build awareness of the way your mind works. By regularly relying on this disciplined practice, you uncover the way you choose to perceive facts, acknowledge your core beliefs, and bear witness to the thoughts and feelings that direct your life. (Remember: Most of our core beliefs are established in our youth, and without examination as an adult, they can unconsciously influence our perception and judgment.)

1. Begin by identifying a situation that is currently challenging you.
2. Write its description as the heading on a page in your journal.

3. Under this heading, write four subheadings: Facts, Beliefs, Thoughts, and Feelings. Prepare to answer the italicized questions listed below.
4. After you establish the facts using the question and details below, drill down into each subsequent subheading (Beliefs, Thoughts, and Feelings) by asking yourself, "Why is this so?" Write down all the reasons you can think of. Keep asking why until you can go no further.

Facts—Sensing (S)

At this moment, what are the tangible, objective facts defining my situation?

These are the nonnegotiable, objective truths that others would agree define your current circumstances: the who, the what, the when, and the where ... such as your physical health, your finances, your living conditions, the weather, current world events, and so on. (Note: To uncover all facts, view your situation by standing in another's shoes or ask for another's input. This approach is encouraged because others can often observe your situation more objectively than you.)

Beliefs—Intuition (N)

At this moment, what beliefs do I hold concerning these facts? Why?

Your beliefs are influenced by your educational, cultural, and religious experiences; the family system you grew up in; your academic training; your work environment, and the communities in which you live and play.

Beliefs serve as powerful information filters, as well as catalysts of behavior. Many people go through life not recognizing their core beliefs and how they act as the operating system of their life experience. "I have to be the best/win," and, "I'm not good enough," are two examples of beliefs that fuel problematic thoughts, feelings, and behaviors. As we saw in the ABC stories presented earlier in this chapter, unchecked beliefs can cause us to make poor choices, stay stuck in unhealthy patterns of behavior, and hurt those we love. You cannot live consciously until you recognize and examine the belief systems influencing you. You get to your core beliefs by continuing to ask, "Why do I believe this?" And answering truthfully each time (e.g., "Because I was told ... Because when I was little I saw ... Because my mother, father, sister did ... and that made me believe ...).

Thoughts (T)

At this moment, what am I thinking about this situation? Why?

It is likely that a mix of facts, beliefs, and feelings will surface in response to these queries. This is because thoughts and feelings are influenced by how your mind processes facts through your belief systems. While thoughts, in theory, are rational, logical evaluations of your perceptions, learned patterns of negative thinking are extremely common. According to Dr. Wayne Dyer, almost everyone engages in them. In his book *Excuses Begone!*, Dyer describes these energy-draining, negative thinking patterns as being under the control of a virus of the mind.[11] He offers examples of what this kind of thinking sounds like to warn you against falling under its destructive spell. Here are a few examples: *I'm so dumb! It will take too long. It has never happened before. It's too risky. People cannot be trusted. There is never enough money.* These types of negative thoughts demonstrate the powerful influence of one's beliefs. To optimize your life energy and increase your happiness, it is essential to catch and avoid the patterns of negative or twisted thinking you may have.

Feelings (F)

At this moment, what am I feeling about this situation? Why?

Your present feelings are influenced by your senses, beliefs, and thoughts. According to Robert Plutchik's psycho-evolutionary theory of basic emotions, there are eight basic emotions that influence human behavior.[12] They are: trust, anticipation, joy, surprise, fear, disgust, anger, and sadness. As you drill into the why of your feelings, don't be surprised to find that you back into your thoughts and beliefs. This is because your feelings are the result of what you sense, believe, and think.

Negative feelings are indicators of an opportunity to recheck and adjust your perceptions and judgments. You put your feelings into perspective by being mindful that only you control your facts, beliefs, and thoughts. When you contemplate the drivers behind your feelings before you behave from a place of sheer emotion, it allows you to put space between you and the situation and positions you to behave in the best manner possible.

The SNTF analysis provides a disciplined approach for positive change by strengthening self-awareness and improving your foundation for conscious choice. Therefore, every time you do this SNTF exercise, please be sure to review what you have written in your journal and highlight the insights you glean.

The SElf-Examination (SEE) Method: Making Awareness-Fueled Choices

Making the best possible choices in each moment helps you create the life you want. In the last exercise, you practiced developing awareness of the mental functions—the facts, beliefs, thoughts, and feelings (SNTFs)—driving your behaviors. This exercise develops behavioral awareness—how and why you make the choices that you do.

The SEE Method is a questioning technique that develops your ability to align with your external circumstances while supporting your inner state of personal balance. Figure 9 depicts how your life story expands with each new experience (each what, how, and why) over time. At the end of your life, what remains is *your story*. By strengthening awareness of each sphere of experience, the SEE Method teaches you to embrace the truth of who you are.

Figure 9. How Your Life Story Develops over Time

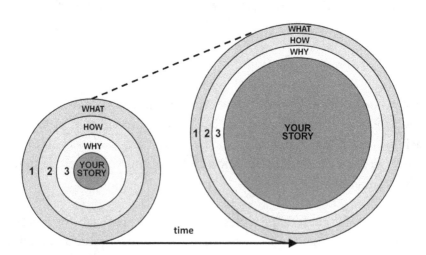

By using three targeted questions, you learn to peel back the onion of your behavior by identifying your thoughts, feelings, and beliefs as situations take place in your life. Disciplining yourself to regularly ask these questions creates a framework of behavioral awareness that supports making your best possible choices.

Each time you employ the SEE Method, you strengthen self-awareness. How well you understand yourself determines your personal power. This is why making a habit of using the SEE Method and providing honest responses to the three questions is essential. Additional information to help you understand each question is provided below, followed by a personal example of the SEE Method.

1. The *outer* circle **What** happened? Identify the situation/triggers/stressors. This circle represents what is happening in your world, your situational triggers—the events/people/environmental/personal factors influencing you. *What* explains the circumstances defining your situation. A few examples: My girlfriend broke up with me. My dog got hit by a car. I got laid off.

2. The *middle* circle **How** did I respond? Identify your behavior and the ACQ you employed. In other words, how did this situation trigger you to act? *How* reminds you to pause and take stock of your behavior, especially during challenging times. Note that no matter the situational context, your response at any specific moment maps to one of the four Authenticity Compass quadrants. (How effectively you employ these skills is a discussion for the next chapter.) The stronger and more accurate your self-awareness is of the quadrant you are tapping into, the more apparent your perceptions and judgments (PJs) will be to you.
3. The *inner* circle **Why** did I respond like this? Identify your SNTFs—the perceptions (facts and beliefs) and judgments (thoughts and feelings) fueling your behavior. Understanding your PJs in the moment is essential to behavior modification and is key to making your life story the story you want it to be. It is essential that you identify the beliefs (especially any limiting ones) that are determining the facts that you are focusing on and that are driving your thoughts and feelings.

SEE Method Personal Example

Pam's Life Experience in 2005, Before SEE

- **What happened?** Rheumatoid arthritis (RA) forced me to stop working in a corporate setting in 2005.
- **How did I respond?** I spent my days managing my pain. I wallowed in self-pity. I was stuck in the present moment and could not envision a meaningful future.
- **Why did I respond like this?** My SNTF analysis was as follows:
  - (S) Facts: I have RA. I am now disabled and cannot work.
  - (N) Beliefs: My identity is defined by my career. Professional status is very important. RA has destroyed my life. I am now worthless.

- o (T) Thoughts: Not being employed means I do not have a meaningful place in society. I do not know if I will have a normal life again.
- o (F) Feelings: I am depressed, hopeless, and angry.

SEE Method Applied

Fast-Forward Ten Years to 2015

- **What happened?** Continually practicing SEE heightened my self-awareness, drove the development of my caretaking skills (Q3), and allowed me to accept the fact that I had to have my knees replaced.
- **How did I respond?** I live an RA-disease-fighting lifestyle. Alongside my regular doctor visits, I benefit from physical therapy, acupuncture, meditation, massage, and an anti-inflammation nutrition plan. When feeling well, I am fully engaged in my personal mission, aligned with my DQ (Q1), to share the Authenticity Compass with others.
- **Why did I respond like this?**
  - o (S) Facts: I have RA. I am still disabled.
  - o (N) Beliefs: Work means more than just making money and having a prestigious job title. It means applying oneself to a meaningful purpose.
  - o (T) Thoughts: I have found my life's purpose and have a mission to teach the benefits of the Authenticity Compass to as many people as I can.
  - o (F) Feelings: I am focused and optimistic.

The following table summarizes how my life improved after I employed the SEE Method and recognized my limiting beliefs.

Table 4. SNTF Analysis: Pre- and Post-SEE Method

SNTF analysis	2005 (pre-SEE)	2015 (post-SEE)
S—Fact	I have RA.	I have RA.
N—My Beliefs	My identity is defined by my career. Professional status is extremely important. RA destroyed my life.	*Work* means more than making money and having a prestigious job title. Work means applying oneself to a meaningful purpose.
T—My Thoughts	Not being employed means I am worthless.	I have a mission to teach the benefits of the AC to as many people as I can.
F—My Feelings	Depressed, angry.	Focused, optimistic.

This personal example shows that even though the *what* (I have RA) did not change from 2005 to 2015, applying the SEE Method changed my beliefs, thoughts, and feelings about the meaning of work and my identity. I began living a more focused, optimistic life as a result of this change in perspective. Strengthening my caretaking skills (my less-dominant quadrant, Q3) allowed me to regain balance and restore strength in my dominant quadrant, Q1.

Exercise 11. The SEE Method: Increasing Behavioral Awareness

The purpose of this exercise is to get insight for positive change by examining your behavior. As you implement SEE, remember: perception drives judgment, judgment drives behavior, and behavior determines results.

Instructions:

Conduct a situational analysis. Do this by first identifying an impactful or stressful situation in your life. Next, using the SEE Method, answer the following questions associated with each one of the three circles in the How Your Life Story Gets Written diagram. Write your responses in your journal.

Step 1. What is happening? Define the situation as accurately as you can. For instance: Who is involved? How did the situation begin? What life domain(s) does it influence? Remember stress is additive. You may, and most likely are, dealing with multiple influencing factors.

Step 2. How am I responding? Document all aspects of your behavior. For example, are you in the grip of negative thinking and emotion? Are you ruminating about the past? Are you worrying about the future? Consider all four quadrants of your Authenticity Compass. Try to identify the quadrant that best explains your behavior. For example, are you applying:

- Q1 skills: Analyzing the situation, thinking things through, planning next steps? (thinking strategically – NT)
- Q2 skills: Springing into action, telling others what to do? (taking action – ST)
- Q3 skills: Demonstrating concern for others? (caring for others – SF)
- Q4 skills: Persuading others to change? (inspiring change – NF)

Stressful times are opportunities for self-awareness. To effectively manage stress, it is necessary to identify its root cause. This is achieved by doing the SNTF analysis in the next step.

Step 3. Why am I responding in this manner? Conduct an SNTF analysis of the situation: Write the four headers—Facts, Beliefs, Thoughts, and Feelings—across the top of a journal page, and list your responses under each heading. Once you have identified all related facts, remember to drill down and ask *why* for each belief, thought, and feeling.

The purpose of this question is to help you develop awareness of who you are by recognizing how your factual reality (S) and beliefs (N) influence your thoughts (T) and your feelings (F). These are the building blocks of your behavior. Understanding the preferences you have for using your PJs helps you understand why you do what you do and the skills you need to develop to eliminate unwanted behaviors, address your weaknesses, and grow.

Changing your behavior requires that you identify the facts and beliefs fueling it. Quite often, belief systems cause the biggest constraints on your path to personal improvement. This is true because belief systems tend to be difficult to identify as well as modify. For example, the belief that worldly success means having a prestigious career and making money kept me stuck in depression and despair until I exchanged it with the belief that success means living a life of purpose (which does not necessarily equate to an impressive job title and salary).

Repeated practice of situational analyses (using the SEE Method) strengthens your self-awareness by revealing the patterns of perception and judgment driving your actions and their subsequent results.

Exercise 12. Putting Positive Change in Motion

You have the power to create positive change. Self-awareness enables you to live the best life possible by guiding you in each moment to the skill sets that best align you with your circumstances and support your personal balance. By successfully achieving a state of alignment and balance, you effectively engage a cycle of success. To maintain it, you must actively listen and respond to constructive feedback (which can come from multiple directions: upstream and downstream in the cycle). Therefore, sustainable success requires honest self-awareness and your continuous attention to feedback. To demonstrate this, the following exercise asks you to employ these principles by exploring a situation from your own life.

Step 1. Select a situation you want to improve in your life and document it in your journal. If others are directly involved in this situation, describe their roles. Now document the following steps and your responses to them.

Step 2. Ask yourself how you are influencing the situation. Apply the SEE Method: What is happening? How am I responding? Why am I responding in this manner? Explore how your perceptions, judgments, and resulting behaviors are contributing to the negativity of the situation in your journal. The following questions may prove helpful. Do you have all the facts? What are they? Are you making excuses, blaming others, or jumping to conclusions? What are your underlying beliefs? Do you have unreasonable expectations? Are your thoughts stuck on a single point? Are your emotions extreme?

Step 3. Determine whether you have a weakness in your PDCA Cycle.

  a. *Map* your behavior in this situation to the Plan-Do-Check-Act Cycle. (See Chapter 2 Exercise 5)

  b. *Identify* the ACQ skills you are relying upon most heavily in this situation.
  Honestly examine your behavior to determine how you may be contributing to misalignment, imbalance, or both. Ask for feedback from others, if applicable.

  c. *Determine* whether there is a "better fit" ACQ.
  Mentally "toggle around" your Authenticity Compass to identify the ACQ skills that might better support alignment and personal balance in this situation. If you are applying your DQ skills, could one of the other three quadrant skills be more appropriate? (It can be helpful to refer to the ACQ Characteristics Table in chapter 1.) Journal your thoughts about the alignment of the situation and the skills needed.

  d. *Apply* skills from the most appropriate ACQ (if there is one).
  If you have difficulty with this step, you most probably need to develop specific skills. Sometimes you can fake it till you make it. In other words, if the needed skills feel unnatural, you develop them by going through the motions until they feel comfortable and reliable.

Step 4. Anticipate and be proactive. Instead of waiting for issues to surface, think ahead about situations and problematic dynamics that are likely to occur. Explore these dynamics by writing about them in your journal. Then:

- Regularly employ the SEE Method.
- Seek feedback when applicable.
- Commit to ACQ toggling and skill development.
- Visualize positive outcomes.

Deming proved that success is achieved by looking at behavior in terms of the PDCA Cycle and by actively managing the feedback that naturally flows between the cycle's four interdependent skill sets.[13] This means that as you start to recognize how every activity and process within your life naturally fits into a Plan-Do-Check-Act Cycle, you will also see that you are regularly taking in new information and learning from it. For example, If you are inspired (*act*) to make a new cake recipe you found in a book, you copy it onto an index card. You make a *plan* to get the right ingredients, pots and pans, and so on, and bring the recipe card into the kitchen to follow (*do*). When the cake is baked, you *check* to see if it tastes good. If it does not taste like you expected, you go back to each step of the process to see where you might have gone wrong. Did you: Copy the recipe correctly (act)? Buy the correct ingredients (plan)? Over or undercook it (do)? We don't normally think about activities in this level of detail, but we are constantly producing and taking in feedback that can support success in every area of our lives.

Actively listening and attending to feedback is key to sustainable process and relationship success whether the process or relationship involves one person, two people, or hundreds of people. If you are wondering how this works, the answer is threefold. First, you use the PDCA framework to get a clear, big picture view of the situation. Second, you recognize when you are stuck in a pattern of success-limiting behavior. (You are if you are impeding the smooth flow of the PDCA Cycle.) Third, you develop the specific skills you need to get unstuck.

Be sure to observe when you are in the grip of negative thinking and emotion in stressful situations. There are two common causes for these unpleasant times. The first is when reliance on your dominant quadrant (DQ) does not support situational alignment or personal balance. The second occurs whenever circumstances demand persistent overreliance on one or more of your less-dominant quadrants (LDQs). Only conscious, committed skill development on your part will help you avoid, or at least minimize, these stressful situations.

Being aware of the behaviors and skills you are employing in the moment alerts you to the ACQ from which you are operating. ACQ awareness improves situations of disharmony and negativity by guiding you to choose PJs that result in positive experiences. Always remember that as long as you are alive, you can choose to create and support alignment and balance in your life.

Chapter 4 Takeaways

- You determine the choices you make from moment to moment that shape your life story.

- How you choose to view and respond to the world—or perceive (sense and intuit) and judge (think and feel)—determines your behavior.

- Your ability to achieve alignment with the people and circumstances in your life and maintain personal balance depends on your ability to make conscious choices.

- You must identify and examine problematic patterns of behavior in your life and the beliefs driving them to make positive changes.

Disciplining yourself to use mental and behavioral awareness methods, such as the SNTF and SEE Methods, will help.

- Create a plan for your best life by thinking about the legacy you want to leave.

- Using your Authenticity Compass helps you develop your self-awareness and life skills so that you can make conscious choices to live the best life possible.

- As long as you are alive, you have options! It is never too late to make changes and choose to experience the happiness and success you deserve.

The self is not something ready-made, but something in continuous formation through choice of action.
—John Dewey

Happiness depends on ourselves.
—Aristotle

None but ourselves can free our minds.
—Bob Marley

CHAPTER 5
PERSONAL SUCCESS

CONNECTING WITH YOUR AUTHENTIC SELF is the first step in defining and achieving personal success. By attaining clarity about your unique purpose, strengths, and growth opportunities, you define your personal success journey. Your Authenticity Compass guides you to understand the truth of who you are, what you want in life, and how to get it. It teaches you how to examine every domain of your life so that you can optimize your purpose and strengths, live in alignment and balance, and achieve sustainable success. By increasing your awareness and authenticity, your Authenticity Compass leads you to the best version of yourself and your happiest and most successful existence.

In this chapter, you will hone in on your true self. Through a Pathway to Authenticity exercise, you will examine the perceptions and judgments influencing each key area of your life and identify the areas you need to work on to achieve personal balance and align with the people and circumstances defining your life. The chapter explains the importance of discovering your purpose, your strengths, and your areas of growth. You then learn how to develop and optimize these success factors to create a working foundation for personal success. An example and an exercise are provided to illustrate how to use your Authenticity Compass to leverage your purpose and strengths, and identify and develop the specific skills you need to create alignment and balance. The chapter concludes with a discussion about how learning to apply the right skills in the right situations, you learn the essential role conscious choice plays in living an authentically happy and successful life.

The meaning of personal success is different for every person. This means what makes you feel successful and happy is unique to you. To define success, you must first connect with your authentic self, the source of your strengths and natural talents. Your authentic self provides the blueprint and direction for your life's purpose and, ultimately, the defining guidance for your happiness and success.

Getting in touch with your authentic self is not always straightforward. This is because as young children we naturally adopt our parents' and caregivers' beliefs and biases about the world, ourselves, and who we are expected to become. The expectations others have about our futures can mark the beginning of a separation from our authentic selves. The media and our families can urge us to define success according to things like the size of our bank accounts, the cost of our homes, the types of cars we drive, and what we do for work. As we grow into adulthood, the mental stronghold these expectations have on us can direct us toward unfulfilling careers, relationships, and experiences. To support our true nature and purpose, we each have a responsibility to ourselves as we mature to examine our belief systems and course correct. Course correction happens when you listen to your inner voice and consistently make choices that keep you in alignment and balance. These choices feel right because they support the well-being of your mind, body, heart, and soul. Choices that cause you to feel bad do not support these positive states of being and cause dis-ease. Staying on a path of alignment and balance is how you achieve your personal definition of success.

Take Daniel, for example. As far back as he can remember, his parents, two successful doctors, expected that he would carry on the family tradition and become a doctor. Once enrolled in college, Daniel, a straight-A high school student, struggled in his biology and chemistry classes. He felt extremely anxious and frequently lost sleep because of his lackluster performance in these premed courses. On the other hand, he passed his elective computer class exams with ease. Being in the computer lab reminded him that he had felt at home around computers since grade school and that he had enjoyed the coding camps he had attended during his summer vacations. After many weeks of internal turmoil, Daniel realized that working toward a degree in computer science was what he wanted to focus on in college.

The night before returning home for his first semester break, Daniel lay awake remembering how he did not enjoy listening to his parents swap stories of their respective emergency and operating room experiences. He wanted to provide helpful and important service to others, just like his parents, but not as a physician. Daniel began visualizing himself at a future UN conference, presenting software he designed to help wealthy nations deliver resources to poor ones. Daniel finally fell asleep dreaming of the good work he could do in the world. He was ready to tell his parents that he would be changing his major from premed to computer science.

Daniel returned home, and after several long and challenging conversations with his parents, he received their permission to switch his college major. Of course, his parents, who believed for so long that Daniel would follow in their footsteps, were shocked by their son's pronouncement. However, as Daniel explained the broad and worthwhile possibilities of a computer-focused career path, his demonstrated enthusiasm and strong academic performance in this area convinced his parents that he was making the right decision.

By choosing a course of study that aligned with his authentic self, Daniel promoted a state of healthy personal balance. His computer science projects gave him joy and satisfaction and resulted in several solid job offers by the time of his graduation. Listening to his inner voice, Daniel positioned himself to provide meaningful service to others while supporting his own personal happiness and sense of success.

Daniel's story demonstrates that connecting with your authentic self often requires calling into question your (and often others') belief systems. When Daniel was on an inauthentic path, it put him into distress mentally, physically, and emotionally, and resulted in poor performance. When Daniel was on the right path, he was in alignment, balance, and flow and was positioned for happiness and success. This story reinforces the importance of listening to and following your inner voice. Your authentic self knows what you need to be happy and successful.

As parents, teachers, employers, and mentors, it is our responsibility to nurture our own authenticity as well as the authenticity of those we guide.

Committing to Personal Authenticity

Personal authenticity means being true to yourself and others. When your facts, beliefs, thoughts, and feelings consistently mirror your words and actions, you are living truthfully. Think of yourself as having two windows:

- an *outside window* that reflects how you present yourself to the world and how others see you based on your choices, words, and actions
- an *inside window* that reflects how you think and feel about yourself. It represents your deepest core beliefs and values

Your authentic self is present when you consciously align these two windows. Unfortunately, many people are not willing to own up to the perceptions, judgments, and choices they make that create the reality they live in. Being authentic and aligning your inside and outside windows requires honesty and effort.

Exercise 13. Your Pathway to Authenticity

The purpose of this exercise is to strengthen your authenticity. By identifying the domains of your life that are presently negatively influencing your alignment with others and/or your ability to experience a sense of personal balance, you pave your way to a happier and more successful life.

The Authenticity Compass

Step 1. Spend the next few minutes in quiet reflection of your current life experience. Identify and list your key domains in your journal. (The eight PLEP domains presented in chapter 2 can assist your thought process.) Be sure to include your key close relationships.

Step 2. Now place a star next to the life domains and relationships that need improvement. These are the areas that cause you the greatest amount of stress, unhappiness, or other negative states of being.

Step 3. For each item with a star, document your answers to these SEE Method questions. (You may want to dedicate at least one page per item.)

- What is happening in this domain/relationship? (Explain the stress.)
- How am I responding to what is occurring?
- Why am I responding like this? (What facts, beliefs, thoughts, and feelings are driving my current behavior? Why?)

Step 4. For each item, identify areas of departure from your authentic self. Spend time answering each of the following questions to assist you in this process:

- In what ways can I be more truthful with myself (and others) within this domain/relationship?
- How can I take more responsibility? What changes in my perceptions (facts, beliefs), judgments (thoughts, feelings), and behaviors can I make in this domain/relationship to better support my true self?
- How can I be more mindful? What different choices can I make to achieve alignment and balance in this domain/relationship (physically, emotionally, mentally, and spiritually)?
- What role, if any, is my DQ playing in this domain/relationship? (Am I overusing my DQ?)
- What skills can I work on to be more successful in this domain/relationship? Where or from whom can I learn them? (Consider the PDCA Cycle at work. Are there any gaps present?)

Step 5. Take time to review the results of this exercise. For each improvement opportunity you identified, add details and time markers to create an improvement plan for yourself. Use a PDCA Cycle to improve each area. Additionally, look for insights, such as recurring themes across your domains. For example, are there multiple issues related to a single belief, feeling, or thought pattern? Is misalignment or imbalance a common cause? It is important to recognize themes or patterns that negatively affect multiple areas of your life. Once you correct them, you improve your life experience in multiple domains.

Living authentically creates the conditions for you to achieve sustainable success and happiness. This involves 1) the continual, honest self-reflection of the facts, beliefs, thoughts, and feelings determining the choices that are influencing your life and those around you, and 2) choosing the perceptions, judgments, and behaviors that achieve purposeful alignment with others while maintaining your personal balance. Your Authenticity Compass supports the aligned positioning of your internal and external windows by teaching you that:

- **Balance demands personal truth.** Being honest with yourself about the work you need to do on skill development, and then doing it, is how you maintain balance in life. As life presents you with challenges, how well you are able to maintain equilibrium and strength (i.e., balance) reveals the degree to which you have (or have not) developed all four ACQ skill sets. Finding ways to develop these skills is necessary to avoid unbalanced states of being when faced with life's challenges.
- **Alignment demands situational truth.** Achieving alignment requires an honest and realistic understanding of the forces influencing you. Only when you accurately identify the facts, beliefs, thoughts, and feelings you hold in a situation (and are open to exploring the facts, beliefs, thoughts, and feelings of others involved in this situation), as well as accept the external forces you cannot change, are you able to make decisions and behave in a manner that promotes alignment in that domain of your life.

Recognizing the external and internal forces (facts, beliefs, thoughts, and feelings) influencing your life and acknowledging your responses to them, positions you to use the PDCA Cycle of Success and put the wheels in motion for improvement and well-being. By regularly applying the PDCA Cycle of Success to each domain of your life, you identify the skill development needed to replace problematic behavior patterns with ones that promote your personal balance and interpersonal alignment.

Your Authenticity Compass supports your personal success journey by showing you how to achieve alignment and balance through conscious choice. You have been provided several Authenticity Compass tools to promote this objective. They include: the Present Life Experience Profile (chapter 2), Applying the PDCA Cycle (chapter 2), the SEE Method (chapter 4), and the Pathway to Authenticity (chapter 5). These exercises are tools that you can use over and over again as you make progress and reassess your next areas of focus. It is essential that you follow through with the plans you make in each exercise. Doing so will strengthen your ability to consciously support your authentic self and your pathway to success.

A common thread between these exercises and all your Authenticity Compass work is growth-oriented self-awareness. This is why establishing a regular form of meditation practice is strongly advocated. It is not by chance that world-class companies and success gurus all around the world promote some form of meditation for increasing energy, developing stamina, making sharp decisions, and managing stress. It is often with a quiet mind that inspiration and creative solutions are born. By applying the ABCs of Authenticity with a quiet mind, you strengthen your ability to consciously choose personal balance and purposeful alignment with others. Trust that your commitment to authenticity will bring you happiness and success. The more you apply the ABCs, the more apparent the evidence will become that you are on the right path.

Identifying Your Authenticity Compass Success Factors

Achieving personal success requires knowing how to create the best possible outcomes in life. You do this by developing clarity about who you are and what you want in life and by choosing alignment and balance. This section describes the three critical success factors you must understand to optimize the use of your Authenticity Compass. They are

1. clarity of your *purpose*,
2. understanding and applying your *strengths*, and
3. identifying and developing your opportunities for *growth*.

Each of these success factors are intimately related to one another. So, as each is discussed below, the relationships between them are also explained.

1. Clarity of Your Purpose

Identifying your purpose in life and choosing activities that support it are essential elements of your personal success journey. Your Authenticity Compass promotes clarity of purpose by guiding you to identify your strengths (your DQ) and your potential growth opportunities (your LDQs) and by encouraging conscious choice in each domain of your life. To achieve your purpose, you must leverage your strengths (the mental functions, behaviors, and skills that come naturally to you) and make a commitment to growth (ongoing skill development). This is what is required to align with your external world, maintain your sense of inner balance, and ultimately achieve flow in your life.

When seeking clarity of purpose, it is important to recognize what you are passionate about. Indicators about your purpose in life come from inner knowledge of what you love to do, what you value, what you are good at (your abilities, skills, etc.), and what you want in life. It is essential, therefore, to take stock of what you know about yourself. Start

The Authenticity Compass

by writing down what you know so far. Use your journal to describe the following:

- What does success mean to you? Why?
- Identify times when you felt happiest and most successful. What were you doing? With whom? What is the common thread?
- What people and things do you value most in life? What do you value most about yourself?
- What are your strengths, abilities, and skills? (Consider your DQ and LDQs.)
- What activities make you feel most fulfilled or put you in a state of flow?
- What do you really want to do? If you already know your purpose and the goals you want to achieve, write them down with as much detail as possible.

As you contemplate your responses to the above-listed questions, it benefits you to consider the contribution or service areas you are passionate about. Research has shown that service to others supports a sense of purpose and has profound mental, physical, spiritual, and emotional benefits.[1] When you think about it, most successful businesses and organizations, large and small, at their core, serve a purpose greater than themselves. For example, Mark Zuckerberg, founder of Facebook, in a 2017 commencement address to Harvard graduates, said, "Our purpose tends to sit in the intersection of what we care about most, and where we can contribute most to helping others."

Many philosophers and scholars believe we have the perfect coding within us to achieve our life's purpose. Understanding your authentic self is the key to decoding your personal success. This is why the Pathway to Authenticity exercise is important. Aligning the windows between your internal and external selves and living mindfully create the required environment for personal success. In addition, a thoughtful review of your legacy exercise (chapter 4) can provide meaningful insight about your path forward.

2. Understanding and Applying Your Strengths

Your DQ: Mental Function and Behavioral Strengths

The Authenticity Compass establishes the relationship between mental functions and the PDCA Cycle of Success. Your Authenticity Compass's dominant quadrant (DQ) is made up of your preferred perception-judgment pair (NT, ST, SF, or NT) and its corresponding Plan-Do-Check-Act success-promoting behavior. Your DQ is your hard-wired area of mental function strength. It translates to the area of behavioral skills that comes most naturally to you. Your DQ skills are typically easier for you to employ than the skills of the other three ACQs. When you identify your DQ, you also identify your three less-dominant quadrants (LDQs), which, when developed, strengthen your ability to address diverse circumstances and manage stress. This is why it is critical to develop the skills of your three LDQs and why growth and learning are intimately linked to your strengths.

Knowing your strengths gives you the information you need to support your purpose and discover the activities that provide fulfillment and ultimately put you into flow, an optimal state of being. Understanding how your DQ has influenced your life experience thus far provides insights into how to leverage it in your future. For example, my friend who recently determined she has a Q3 DQ (sensing-feeling/caretaking) had a big aha moment when she connected it to her career in nursing and lifelong pursuit of caregiving in various settings. She then realized that her dissatisfaction with her life was not related to her purpose and strengths in caregiving, which she was in alignment with, but was actually related to her current job, which was creating imbalance on a regular basis.

This information helped her realize she had to choose to move on to a new work environment that would allow her to experience more balance and flow or to learn specific skills (of her LDQs) to help her cope with the ongoing challenges of her current workplace. However, before she figured out her DQ, she was considering changing careers altogether, which likely would have totally put her out of alignment with her purpose and made it very difficult for her to experience balance and flow. Without realizing it, many people make the wrong choices for the wrong reasons and end up unable to lead fulfilling lives. This is why understanding and leveraging your DQ strengths is critical in fulfilling your purpose in life.

Table 5 provides guidance for understanding and applying your DQ strengths as well as potential areas for growth. For each DQ listed in the first column, strengths associated with it are listed in the second column. The most common areas requiring skill development for a specific DQ are found in its opposite quadrant and are known as its blind spot. (See the third column.) The two other LDQs also typically present opportunities for skill development and are found in the quadrants positioned next to one's DQ. (See the last column.) Therefore, when you know a person's DQ, you know three things:

1. their innate *natural strengths* (their DQ skills),
2. their *most likely weakness or blind spot* (the skills associated with the LDQ directly opposite their DQ), and
3. their *other potential skill development areas* (the skills associated with the LDQs adjacent to their DQ).

Use the following table for guidance when attempting to understand your or another's DQ strengths and skill development / growth opportunities.

Table 5. Strengths and Skill Development Opportunities by DQ

Dominant Quadrant (DQ)	Natural Strengths for This DQ	Likely Skill Development Needs (Blind Spot)	Other Potential Growth Areas (Adjacent LDQs)
Q1 NT/Plan *intuitive-thinking*	**Planning/ Designing** Future-oriented. Sees big picture. Has vision; uses strategy and logic. Focuses on how it all fits together.	**Q3:** Sensing-feeling skills (caretaking/monitoring) Being in the present. Focusing on details and what matters to people. Providing sympathy and support. Developing effective monitoring/caretaking skills.	**Q2:** Doing what is needed to execute a plan. Using tangible facts in decision-making. Being hands-on and task/ action/results-oriented. **Q4:** Motivating and inspiring others. Focusing on possibilities. Social skills. Empathy. Involving people/ gaining their commitment.
Q2 ST/Do *sensing-thinking*	**Building/ Implementing** Present-oriented. Hands-on; action-focused; results-driven. Fact-based; stable. Sees details, tasks. Focuses on doing what is needed to execute a plan.	**Q4:** Intuitive-feeling skills (motivating/ inspiring change) Embracing future thinking and planning activities. Focusing on possibilities. Social skills; empathy. Involving people/gaining their commitment.	**Q1:** Seeing the big picture and how it all fits together. Using logic and strategy. Having vision; understanding strategy. **Q3:** Focusing on details and what matters to people. Providing sympathy and support. Developing effective monitoring/caretaking skills.
Q3 SF/Check *sensing-feeling*	**Monitoring/ Caretaking** Present-oriented. Sympathetic and supportive. Harmonizer; has effective monitoring skills. Focuses on details and what matters to people.	**Q1:** Intuitive-thinking skills (planning/ designing) Embracing future thinking and planning activities. Focusing on how it all fits together; seeing the big picture; having vision. Using logic and strategy.	**Q4:** Motivating and Inspiring others. Focusing on possibilities. Social skills; empathy. Involving people/ gaining their commitment. **Q2:** Doing what is needed to execute a plan. Using tangible facts in decision-making. Being hands-on, task/action/results-oriented.
Q4 NF/Act *intuitive-feeling*	**Motivating/ Inspiring Change** Future-oriented. Has strong social skills; empathy. Involves people/gains their commitment. Innovative; insightful; has vision. Focuses on possibilities and enabling change.	**Q2:** Sensing-thinking skills (building/ implementing) Being in the present. Focusing on doing what is needed to execute a plan. Embraces details. Being hands-on; task/ action/results-oriented. Fact-based; stable.	**Q1:** Seeing the big picture and how it all fits together. Using logic. Understanding strategy. **Q3:** Focusing on details and what matters to people. Providing sympathy and support. Developing effective monitoring/ caretaking skills.

Your Character Strengths

Character strength awareness combined with the awareness of your DQ strengths provides an even stronger foundation for your personal authenticity and a basis for your success journey. The more you commit to truly knowing yourself, the stronger your sense of meaning and purpose becomes and the better positioned you are to overcome obstacles and achieve your goals. Recognizing your character strengths will 1) help you better understand what makes you unique by explaining the capabilities you have ready access to in any situation, 2) strengthen your sense of alignment and balance by supporting the optimal use of your ACQ skills, and 3) help you clarify the behavioral differences you witness in individuals who share the same DQ as you.

You are encouraged to identify your top character strengths to have quick access to your best and strongest traits. These indicate what you deeply care about in life and how your values influence the choices you make that contribute to your happiness and success. Internalizing your character strengths encourages you to become the best version of yourself because they reinforce what brings you happiness and provide helpful guideposts on your path to personal success.

Through groundbreaking research, the VIA Institute has identified twenty-four character strengths that represent the best characteristics of humanity. Three examples are honesty, kindness and gratitude. In their book, *The POWER of Character Strengths,* Ryan M. Niemiec and Robert E. McGrath, leaders of the VIA Institute, provide a comprehensive review of all twenty-four.[2] I believe those of you who explore your character strengths will find, as I have, that character strength knowledge enhances the development of ACQ skills.

A good way to obtain a view of your character strengths is by taking a complimentary web-based survey provided by the VIA Institute on Character (https://viacharacter.org/www/Character-Strengths-Survey). The VIA Institute on Character regularly publishes new findings from their latest research on character strengths and is a great resource for more information on this topic. Additionally, if you are interested in studying character strengths and their application, the following book is strongly recommended: *30 Days of Character Strengths: A Guided Practice to Ignite Your Best* by Jane S. Anderson.[3]

Identifying and Developing Your Opportunities for Growth

Change is a constant in life. This is why it is important to be willing to learn the skills needed to meet new challenges while staying on course with your authentic self. It is essential to your growth as a human being to develop the skills of all four Authenticity Compass quadrants. This is especially true if you want to experience balance and alignment with the people and circumstances you encounter in life.

When you determine your Authenticity Compass's area of strength (your DQ), you also learn your three less-dominant quadrants (your LDQs), which are areas where you are likely to require skill development. Using table 5, you can get an idea of the specific skills associated with each ACQ and begin to prioritize a growth plan. As your purpose, vision, and goals become clearer, the skills you need to develop will become more domain- and subject-specific.

As you pursue your purpose, applying PDCA Cycles will help you uncover the growth and improvement opportunities you need to succeed. By actively listening and applying the feedback you obtain from your PDCA Cycles, you will create new relationships, develop new skills, and gain experience.

Optimizing Your Success

You experience success by choosing alignment and balance and by optimizing the critical success factors of Authenticity Compass use: embrace your purpose, apply your strengths, and develop your opportunities for growth. The following table provides a framework for examining your opportunities for growth.

The Authenticity Compass

Table 6. Promoting Alignment, Balance, and Success

The Problem	My Beliefs/ Actions	Primary ACQ/ PDCA Activity I'm Applying/	Feedback (External Perspective)	PDCA Weakness/ Better Choice ACQ, Why?

Your personal and professional success require you to recognize the effect your behavior is having on you and on others. Your understanding of the interpersonal dynamics defining your life domains must be accurate and complete to make choices that keep you on a successful life path.

Exercise 14. Creating Your Plan for Success

The purpose of this exercise is to create your plan for success. You do this by documenting your purpose, strengths, and the growth opportunities that will strengthen alignment and balance in your life.

Begin by answering the following questions:

Purpose

- Do I have clarity of purpose?
- Am I aligned with my purpose?"

If the answer is no to either of these questions, revisit the Clarity of Your Purpose section under Identifying Your Authenticity Compass Success Factors.

Strengths

- Do I understand my strengths?
- Do I apply my strengths?

If the answer is no to either of these questions, revisit the Understanding and Applying Your Strengths section. If you have not Identified your DQ, revisit chapter 1.

Growth Opportunities

When you identify the PDCA Cycle weaknesses (i.e. the ACQ skill development opportunities) that exist in your life, you identify dynamics

The Authenticity Compass

contributing to misalignment and imbalance. Here are step-by-step directions to analyze the areas of your life that are presently problematic:

1. Table 6 is provided to guide your thinking. You might want to recreate Table 6 in your journal.
2. Identify any specific relationships or activities in your life that you are struggling with. Dedicate one row to each.
3. Complete each field of the table for each specific relationship or activity identified. You can refer to table 5 to select ACQs to complete the last column.
4. After you fill out the table, create a list of insights and action items. Consider how misalignments and imbalances may be connected and whether you have identified opportunities to develop any specific LDQ skills.
5. Once you become comfortable with this exercise, plan to revisit it on a regular basis. Be sure to follow through on the improvements you identify. Developing all four ACQ skill sets and choosing the best skill set for each situation you face enables you to establish alignment and balance in your life.

The connections that exist between your success factors—purpose, strengths, and growth opportunities—reinforce the relationship that exists between the choices you make, who you are, and the impact you have on the world. You honor your gift of life energy by committing to your authentic self. This commitment requires continual, honest self-evaluation, the essential precursor to alignment, balance, and flow (your optimal state of being). If you are finding it difficult to get started, *remind yourself of these Authenticity Compass Principles*:

- **Stay mindful.** Awareness of your authentic self requires a peaceful mind. Daily meditation, breathing techniques, journaling, coloring, and walks in nature are just a few effective ways to quiet your thoughts so that you can look inward for guidance.
- **Live by the ABCs of Authenticity (choose alignment and balance) to achieve success and happiness.** You are in control of your perceptions (sensing and beliefs) and judgments (thoughts

and feelings). By making the best choices available to you in each moment, you will live your best possible life and avoid living in regret.
- **Apply the Plan-Do-Check-Act Cycle of Success to each domain of your life.** Consciously employ the skills of all four Authenticity Compass quadrants to what matters most to you (e.g., your marriage, your children, your career, your health, etc.). Identify, appreciate, and support (through skill development) the interdependencies that exist between all four quadrants in each of your life domains. Discard the beliefs, thoughts, feelings, and behaviors that don't serve you.

Chapter 5 Takeaways

- Living authentically creates the conditions for success and happiness. Your authentic self is the source of your talents, your true purpose, and your blueprint for success.

- You have a responsibility to find your path to authentic personal success so you can contribute your unique gifts to the world. You do this by developing your self-awareness, examining your belief systems, and correcting your life course as needed.

- You develop self-awareness by applying your Authenticity Compass to each domain of your life. This teaches you to make conscious choices about:
  - The perceptions (facts and beliefs) and judgments (thoughts and feelings) that drive your behavior
  - How your behavior affects your life, others and the planet

- You achieve your personal definition of success by continually making conscious choices to support your alignment and balance.

The Authenticity Compass

- Applying the PDCA Cycle to a problematic area of your life ensures you make use of external feedback to identify your opportunities for improvement.

- By committing to the following Authenticity Compass success factors, you put yourself on a path to authentic success and happiness.
  o Establish clarity of purpose.
  o Understand and apply your strengths.
  o Identify and address your growth opportunities.

- Adopting a meditation practice reinforces your commitment to truth, responsibility, and mindfulness and thereby, strengthens your ability to employ the ABCs of Authenticity.

It takes courage to grow up and
become who you really are.
—E. E. Cummings

The meaning of life differs from man to man,
from day to day and from hour to hour. What
matters, therefore, is not the meaning of life
in general but rather the specific meaning
of a person's life at a given moment.
—Viktor Frankl, MD

Your time is limited, so don't waste
it living someone else's life.
—Steve Jobs

CHAPTER 6
AUTHENTICITY COMPASS APPLICATIONS

UNDERSTANDING HOW TO MANAGE SITUATIONS that challenge your sense of alignment and balance in life is essential to your well-being. The purpose of this chapter is to strengthen your responses to life's challenges by providing you with four Authenticity Compass applications: blind spot management, relationship harmony, Backward-4 decision-making, and ICE-ing (identify/cope/exit-ing). By fortifying your self-awareness and advocating conscious choice, these applications improve your communication and stress management skills and, ultimately, your personal and professional relationships.

Using these applications requires knowing your Authenticity Compass DQ. To receive maximum benefit from the applications that pertain to your relationships, it is important to identify the DQs of the people with whom you interact. Therefore, it is recommended that you dedicate some journal time to documenting what you believe to be the dominant Authenticity Compass quadrants of the significant people in your life (i.e., your spouse, boss, children, best friend, etc.). You can use the ACQ Characteristics Table in chapter 1 to guide your educated guess (which is sufficient for your initial work with these AC applications) or, ideally, have the significant people in your life identify their own DQs using the instructions in chapter 1's, exercise 1.

Application 1: Blind Spot Management

Operating with a blind spot means you are making a decision or taking action without having all the information you need. An Authenticity Compass–defined blind spot means you are operating with a perception-judgment (PJ) weakness. This means either your perception of a situation is not totally accurate, your reaction to it is biased, or both. Your blind spot is typically located directly opposite your DQ and, by definition, requires skill development. For example, before I recognized that I had a Q3 blind spot and developed caretaking skills to support this quadrant, I easily fell into behavior patterns that were counterproductive to my health and my relationships. I could be entrenched in my DQ (Q1) and work at my desk for hours without regularly getting up and stretching. I now have the awareness and self-caregiving skills to take better care of my arthritic joints. My blind spot would also unintentionally affect members of my family at times when I would offer them strategic advice (Q1) instead of recognizing and attending to their emotional needs (Q3).

Because it is highly likely that you (and everyone you know) have an Authenticity Compass blind spot, it is positively life-changing when you choose to consciously address it. By doing so, you become better prepared to participate in challenging interpersonal interactions and avoid behaving in ways that you later regret.

How to Identify Your Blind Spot

Consider your potential DQ blind spot by reviewing the following facts:

- If your DQ is Q1 (you prefer future-oriented, conceptual, intuitive-thinking), you most likely favor planning activity over in-the-moment, sensing-feeling, caretaking activity (Q3) and likely have a Q3, caretaking blind spot.
- If your DQ is Q3 (you prefer to be engaged in present-state, fact-based feeling activities), you most likely favor in-the-moment caretaking over future, intuitive-thinking, planning activities (Q1) and likely have a Q1, planning blind spot.
- If your DQ is Q2 (you prefer present-state, factual thinking), you most likely prefer doing over inspiring change, which is a future-oriented conceptual/intuitive-feeling activity (Q4), and likely have

The Authenticity Compass

a Q4 blind spot when it comes to being motivated or motivating others.
- If your DQ is Q4 (you prefer future-oriented conceptual, intuitive feeling), you most likely favor inspiring change over a present-state, factual-thinking doing/implementing activity (Q2) and likely have a Q2, doing/implementing blind spot.

Blind spots are revealed when you become aware of the skill development gaps that exist in your less-dominant quadrants (LDQs), especially the LDQ opposite your DQ. Chapter 3's stories (the scholar, hero, benevolent leader, and lover) were presented as extreme examples of the imbalance in behavior that can occur when one operates with one or more blind spots and when the energy of the dominant quadrant is employed to the near-exclusion of the other three quadrants. Figure 10 depicts the story of the scholar (Q1) who is so rigidly entrenched in his intuitive-thinking (NT) planning DQ that he is unable to accept the facts (S) associated with collaborative technology or understand the feelings (F) of his students. His DQ (Q1) is shaded. The triangle symbol denotes his Q3 blind spot. His two other LDQs are represented by an *X*.

Figure 10. The Scholar Blind Spot Example

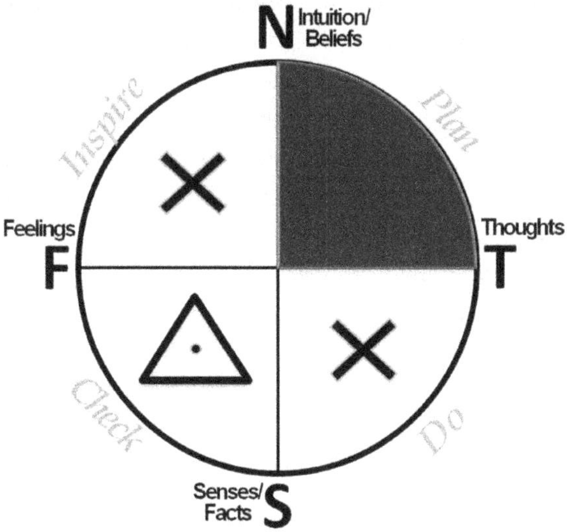

Operating from your dominant quadrant is completely natural and quite easy to do. However, if you rely primarily on your DQ, you run the risk of operating with a blind spot. The best way to avoid this behavioral dilemma is to develop skills that support all four Authenticity Compass quadrants, especially the one opposite your DQ (your potential blind spot). As has already been explained, this quadrant most likely represents your least developed skill base.

Improving your life and your relationships demands behavioral self-awareness and skill development. It takes maturity and the regular self-assessment of your thoughts, feelings, and actions to effectively identify and expand your less-dominant skill bases.

Exercise 15. Blind Spot Investigation

The purpose of this exercise is to help you develop awareness about how your blind spot may be contributing to negative states of being in your life and to identify skills you can develop to create alignment and balance.

Step 1. Find your DQ in table 7. Using the descriptions as a guide, think about a situation or interaction in your life where your behavior is or was less than ideal and results in stress.

Step 2. Document this situation or interaction in your journal using the same thinking as in the table column headers. ("I was doing this when the situation called for that.") Do this as factually as possible, and do not judge yourself. Remember, our LDQ skills do not always feel natural to us, so when we are put in situations where they are needed, if we have not yet developed an LDQ skill base, we can find ourselves behaving suboptimally.

Table 7. Why Your Go-To Behaviors May Not Produce Desired Results

Your DQ	You may have been:	... when the situation called for:
Q1	planning far ahead, overthinking things, too analytical and logical	the monitoring and caretaking of self and others; sympathy and empathy (Q3: sensing-feeling, SF/Check skills)
Q2	too hands-on, overdoing it, going too fast, laser-focused on the details of the task at hand	big-picture thinking, delegating tasks, motivating others to participate (Q4: intuitive-feeling NF/Act skills)
Q3	smothering others, intrusive, acting as a helicopter parent/spouse/boss/etc.	planning ahead/strategizing, logical analysis (Q1: intuitive-thinking, NT/Plan skills)
Q4	imagining too far out of the box, too focused on aesthetics	focus on details and down-to-earth tasks, actions with measurable outcomes (Q2: sensing-thinking, ST/Do skills)

Step 3. Now answer the following questions in your journal:

- How did the quadrant opposite your dominant quadrant play a role in the situation, if any? Did it or another ACQ act as a blind spot?
- How did your DQ influence (help or hurt) the situation or interaction? (Are you overreliant on it?)
- Now imagine the same situation or interaction with you employing the skills of an ACQ that could have produced a better outcome. Which quadrant is it? Why is this a better fit?
- What skills do you now know you need to develop? How can you learn these skills and practice their use so you can achieve alignment and balance in this situation and others like it going forward?

Blind Spot Management Key Learning Points

It is likely you have underdeveloped skills or a "blind spot" in one or more of your less-dominant quadrants (LDQs). If this is the case, it is important to realize your blind spot can negatively affect the circumstances and relationships important to you. By developing skills that address your blind spots (i.e., ultimately by developing all four ACQ skill sets), you can significantly improve your relationships, especially the challenging ones. This is certainly the case when the people you depend upon (or who depend upon you) have DQs and blind spots that differ from yours.

Application 2: Relationship Harmony

Every person has an Authenticity Compass dominant quadrant (DQ) that represents their preferred way of viewing and responding to the world. Conflicts between individuals often arise because they perceive and judge the same circumstance differently. The purpose of the Relationship Harmony Application is to minimize conflict by providing an understanding of how each set of dominant quadrants interact. DQ awareness provides an effective platform for relationship harmony by expanding your understanding of how differences in perception and judgment influence your interactions.

What Motivated Me to Study Relationship Harmony?

I became curious about the drivers of human behavior at a young age because I grew up in a home where there was much love but also continual conflict. My father, an accountant, was an athletic, fun-loving man who worked as a handyman and property maintenance fellow at night and on weekends. He was a sensitive, family-oriented father who freely applied his time and diverse fix-it skills to the homes of his friends and large extended family. My mother, a nurse and strict disciplinarian, held high expectations for her life and developed deep resentment for my father's inability to say no when others asked for his help. As a result of her parenting, I learned self-discipline, the importance of academic standing, and the role status plays in society. I learned generosity and zest for life from my father. My greatest lesson, however, came as a result of my mother's death when I was fourteen. She left me pondering a terribly difficult question: How can two people (my parents) love each other and yet be in a continual state of conflict? Decades after my mother's passing, I found an answer in Carl Jung's writings that finally made sense of my parents' interactions and gave me a sense of closure.

Jung's description of the differences in how people perceive and judge their circumstances not only helps explain my parents' continual discord but also offers harmony-promoting advice for all relationships. By studying Jung's work, I realized my parents had opposing dominant quadrants. My father was a strong sensing-feeler (Q3). He lived in the moment and was driven by his desire to help others. My mother was a strong intuitive-thinker (Q1). She was a planner, always thinking about the future and analyzing the cause and effect of my father's behavior (as well as everyone else's in the family). Perception-judgment differences fueled their struggle to establish alignment and balance in their relationship and in our home. The following interaction example demonstrates how my parents' opposing DQs fostered arguments.

Family and friends always turned to my father when their homes had an electrical, plumbing, or carpentry problem or needed some other improvement. His giving nature made it impossible for him to refuse their cries for help, and once engaged in a task, he easily lost track of time. His concern for others and his poor time management skills (which resulted in perpetual tardiness) were constant sources of frustration for my mother, who continued to plan our family dinners as well as their social activities with friends. My father found it difficult to understand her profound frustration with his behavior because he believed helping others (his Q3 focus) took precedence over punctuality and adherence to a predefined schedule (her Q1 focus).

Ultimately, harmony was elusive in our home because my parents (like most people) were DQ-unaware. They had no clue that their preferred ways of perceiving and responding to life's challenges were fundamentally different. My mother wanted her needs and the needs of our home to have top priority. In my father's heart, they always did, but because of his continual overcommitment to others, they rarely did in practice.

Minimizing and Eliminating Conflict

Jung's research and the subsequent work of Carolyn Zeisset[1] prove knowing your natural tendencies for perceiving and responding to others enables you to minimize, if not prevent, interpersonal conflict. Flavil R. Yeakly's research[2] provides three reasons for why this is so. Here they are, presented in Authenticity Compass terms:

1. Communication is usually *easy* between you and someone who has the *same* dominant quadrant as you do.
2. Communication is usually *moderately difficult* between you and someone who has a dominant quadrant *adjacent* to your dominant quadrant.
3. Communication is usually *difficult* between you and someone who has a dominant quadrant *opposite* your dominant quadrant.

The following pages discuss the communication dynamics of each interacting set of DQs in more detail. Keep your journal handy so that you can note when an important relationship in your life maps to one of the communication dynamics described. The point of this journaling effort is to identify—in each relationship where conflict exists—the interaction skills that can foster alignment between you and another and avoid the emotional imbalance relationship conflict causes. While you cannot change another person's behavior, having DQ awareness (of your and the other person's DQ) can guide you to consciously choose words and actions that promote, rather than discourage, harmony. DQ awareness also reinforces the fact that developing the skills of all four Authenticity Compass quadrants is critical for achieving alignment in all the relationships in your life.

The Authenticity Compass

You Have the Same DQs: Why Communication Is Usually Easy

Both of you perceive the world in a similar way (which means you both prefer either *sensing* or *intuiting* as the primary way to gather information from your environment), *and* you both respond to the world in a similar way (which means you both prefer either *thinking* or *feeling* as the primary driver of your decisions). Given that you share the same intrinsic skill sets, you may also share similar passions, areas of study, or careers. The statement, "We are like two peas in a pod," aptly describes the nature of this type of interpersonal relationship. Can you think of someone you believe shares the same dominant quadrant as you? What are the defining characteristics and skills that lead you to this conclusion? (Remember, however, that the P and J axes are continuums, so it is possible for two people to have the same DQ but still experience the world differently and have interaction challenges.)

You Have Adjacent DQs: Why Communication Can Be Moderately Difficult

In this case, one of your ACQ coordinates is the same as the person you are interacting with, and one ACQ coordinate is different. This means you either share the way you perceive (*sense* or *intuit*) *or* the way you judge (*think* or *feel*). Table 8 documents the four possible scenarios of adjacent DQs and the conflicts you can expect when you share only one ACQ coordinate with someone else.

Table 8. Interpersonal Conflict Summary for Adjacent DQs

The Interacting DQs	Shared Preference	Potential Conflict
Q1 and Q4	Intuition (N)	Conflict of Judgment: (Thinking vs. Feeling)
Q2 and Q3	Sensing (S)	Conflict of Judgment: (Thinking vs. Feeling)
Q1 and Q2	Thinking (T)	Conflict of Perception: (Intuition vs. Sensing)
Q3 and Q4	Feeling (F)	Conflict of Perception: (Intuition vs. Sensing)

To help illustrate this type of conflict, here is an anecdote from my life. Whenever my husband (Q2) and I (Q1) disagree, it never ceases to amaze me to find our conflict is fueled by my focus being on the future (intuition) and his focus being on the present (sensing). For example, at dinnertime when our children were young, my husband believed our children should eat everything on their plates before they could be excused from the table. My thoughts about the potential future implications of this fairly common discipline—specifically my concern about the possible creation of eating disorders—frequently made this dinner-table practice stressful for me. Take a moment to think about your own experiences with relationship conflict.

The following four cases provide additional detail regarding the types of conflict that can occur when you are interacting with someone whose dominant quadrant is adjacent to yours. These cases demonstrate why communication is likely to be moderately difficult when you share only one perception-judgment coordinate.

Conflicts of Judgment: *Thinking versus Feeling*

Case A: Q1 and Q4 Interaction Conflict

When you and a friend, colleague, or family member share intuition (N) as your dominant mode of perception, it means you both prefer to focus on the big picture and may overlook the details. At the same time, because you do not share the same preference for judgment, it means you are likely to differ in your reactions to people and situations. One of you may be driven by cognitive intelligence / rational thought (T) and the other by emotional intelligence / the feelings (F) of the people involved.

Here is an example: You and two friends go shopping. You try on a dress and ask your friends what they think. Friend A, an intuitive *thinker* (Q1), says bluntly, "The dress does nothing for you apart from the color being attractive. It makes you look like an old lady." Friend B, an intuitive *feeler* (Q4), jumps in, choosing her words carefully. She says,

"The color is amazing on you! I just wish the dress enhanced your shape a little more. Maybe we can find one that does."

As shown in the above example, individuals with a Q1 preference tend to demonstrate truthful, cut-to-the-chase communication styles (which can be effective and often preferred in business settings). People with a Q1 preference must often work harder than people with an intuitive feeling (Q4) preference to employ tact in their interactions. In Q1-Q4 interactions, it is helpful to pay attention to the details and to focus on the present moment to minimize conflict.

Case B: Q2 and Q3 Interaction Conflict

Sharing a preference for sensing (S) means you both prefer to focus on the details versus the big picture. It also means you both tend to focus on the present versus the future. Additionally, you will find there tends to be differences in how the two of you make decisions and respond to challenges. To illuminate this fact, let's consider the dynamics in a home with young children where one parent is a sensing *feeler* (Q3) and the other is a sensing *thinker* (Q2). In this household, it is likely the parents' child-rearing techniques are markedly different. The parent with a thinking preference (T) is more likely to embrace rules and be a consistent disciplinarian, whereas the parent with the feeling preference (F) may be more flexible and gentler in approach.

Understanding the built in T-F polarity of a relationship helps couples avoid energy-draining struggles concerning the upbringing of their children. (Disagreements regarding discipline are common.) Potential arguments can be prevented by discussing one's preference for disciplinary tactics and by creating a mutually agreed upon game plan before taking on a coparenting role. Without doing so, one of you may find yourself in the role of the sole disciplinarian. This is not only unfair but is also likely to cause frequent relationship conflicts. Identifying the T-F conflict for what it is can, at the very least, lessen the confrontations that occur between parents.

Proactively discussing the implications of a judging preference difference (thinking versus feeling) will strengthen any relationship, whether personal or professional. Reaching consensus about where your ideas diverge and how and when decisions are made are keys to relationship harmony. To minimize conflict in Q2-Q3 interactions, be sure to pay attention to the big picture and plan for the future together.

Conflicts of Perception: *Intuition versus Sensing*

Case C: Q1 and Q2 Interaction Conflict

When you and someone else share a preference for thinking (T), it means you both rely upon logical reasoning in your decision-making. However, if you do not also share the same perceiving function, it is likely you differ in how you view the world. The reason being one of you is oriented to the big picture or vision (N), and the other gravitates toward the details or current facts (S). When this is the case (as it is with my husband and me), it is common to find the two of you discussing completely different aspects and implications of the same topic. People who easily see the big picture naturally tend to orient toward the future. People who prefer to concentrate on the facts at hand tend to focus on the present.

Q1 versus Q2 conflicts are often priority related. They occur both in work and personal settings. It is especially important to proactively identify these tension-causing dynamics in your relationships. The intuitive-thinking person, focused on the future, puts energy into planning. The sensing-thinking person, focused on the present, directs energy toward the things that must be attended to right now. To ease conflict within Q1-Q2 interactions, it is especially helpful to clearly define scope and timelines on all projects.

Case D: Q3 and Q4 Interaction Conflict

When feeling (F) is the shared primary judging function, a conflict similar to the previous case (Q1 versus Q2) occurs between Q4 and Q3. Sensing feelers (Q3) tend to be focused on present-state feelings, while intuitive feelers (Q4) tend to be focused on what the future state of feeling could be. Sensing feelers (Q3) typically embrace the role of an empathetic caretaker, whereas intuitive feelers (Q4) tend to be motivating change agents. Both roles are valuable when applied in the right circumstances as demonstrated in the following example.

Your brother discovers his fiancée is cheating on him. He is devastated. He calls you in despair. If you are a sensing feeler (your DQ is Q3), you will most likely commiserate with him over the betrayal and seek ways to bolster his spirits in the present moment (e.g., suggest taking him out to dinner so the two of you can talk face-to-face). If you are an intuitive feeler (your DQ is Q4), your response is likely to focus on the future. You might say, "You are so lucky to have discovered her infidelity before you married her! Can you imagine the mess you would be in if you were married? Cut your losses. Look forward to finding a faithful partner. There are many more fish in the sea, and you are a great catch!"

This example highlights the time orientation difference that exists between sensing feelers (present state) and intuitive feelers (future state). To avoid conflicts between Q4 and Q3, it is essential to understand the differences in perception and time orientation of these DQs. A Q3 sensing feeler is more focused on caretaking in the moment, whereas a Q4 intuitive feeler is more focused on how change will affect the future. Understanding that the different responses of the Q3 and Q4 DQs are innate is the most important part of relationship harmony for this pair. A Q3-Q4 partnership needs to work on prioritization of time and tasks to help ease conflict.

You Have Opposite DQs: Why Communication Tends to Be Difficult

The two of you perceive and respond to the world differently. These blind-spot communications, shown in table 9, can be particularly difficult. As you think about this table, keep in mind the good news. By developing the communication skills of your blind spot, you can minimize conflict in the interactions you have with individuals whose DQ is opposite yours.

Table 9. Conflicts of Opposing Dominant Quadrants (DQs)

Difficult Communication Pair	Explanation: You tend to perceive and respond to the world differently!
Q1 and Q3	future-oriented conceptual thinker vs. present-state fact-based feeler
Q2 and Q4	present-state factual thinker vs. future-oriented conceptual feeler

Increasing Your Interaction Effectiveness

Developing and applying the appropriate ACQ in interactions is key to your alignment and effectiveness. No matter what your DQ is, you can become proficient in all four Authenticity Compass skill sets. (Keep in mind that according to Jung, this is how a person achieves adult maturity.) Specifically, this means at minimum choosing to think in both present and future terms as well as being able to:

- Grasp the big picture and put a plan in place. (Q1 skills)
- Focus on details and follow through on instructions. (Q2 skills)
- Monitor a situation and show concern for others. (Q3 skills)
- Inspire and motivate change. (Q4 skills)

Workplaces can be especially challenging when it comes to human interactions. Role clarity is critical to business performance because each role is a leverage point in the organization's success. Specifically, each handoff within a business environment offers a potential opportunity to improve the way work is being done. If you or others that you work with are not clear about your role (or vice versa), it is extremely difficult to harness opportunities to improve performance. To optimize interactions and improve process performance within your work environment, use these tips:

- Be clear about your job and the skills you need to fulfill it. Your role within your company identifies the AC quadrant skills your workplace requires of you to ensure its success.
- Identify who you are dependent upon to do your work correctly.
- Know who within the workplace is dependent upon you to accomplish their work.
- As you move clockwise around the PDCA Cycle that defines the work being done within your team or group, identify the handoffs. Then, have each person making a handoff ask the following two questions of the handoff receiver:

  1. What do you need from me? (Identify any gaps between what is needed and what is being provided.)
  2. What will you do with what I give you? (This question can reveal something else the giver can provide that will better serve the receiver's needs.)

It will prove beneficial to your personal and professional relationships to learn the most effective ways to interact with and influence people who have a different DQ than you. The following DQ-based guidance is offered to help you maintain better balance and achieve greater states of alignment in your interactions.

Influencing an Intuitive Thinker (NT) / Planner **(Q1)**

You must be seen as a credible source of information because people with Q1 as their DQ are typically focused on competency, strategy, theory, and research. Remember Q1s are big-picture thinkers who intuitively form an integrated, holistic view of the subject being discussed. To strengthen your rapport with Q1s, be prepared to discuss future possibilities (especially broad, far-reaching ones), and, whenever possible, provide them with logical alternatives.

Influencing a Sensing Thinker (ST) / Doer *(Q2)*

Individuals with Q2 as their DQ like to be shown how things work. They tend to be practical people who focus on results and getting things done efficiently. Depending on the subject matter of your interaction, be prepared to discuss details such as why something is a good idea, how a plan translates into specific actions, and how the results will be measured. It is also especially important to answer all questions a Q2 asks. Therefore, before you interact, think about the most likely fact-based questions you will be asked. To influence a Q2, your answers need to reflect logical, analytical, and quantitative thinking.

Influencing a Sensing Feeler (SF) / Checker *(Q3)*

Q3 individuals appreciate personal interactions and tend to put them into a personal context. Therefore, in your discussions it is important to demonstrate respect (for them and any others you refer to). They are motivated by benefits and would rather hear them explicitly stated than implied. Q3s appreciate personal testimonials so, wherever possible, use them in your discussions. Lastly, remember that Q3s prefer to focus on practical and immediate results.

Influencing an Intuitive Feeler (NF) / Motivator *(Q4)*

Q4s are adept motivators of people. They value exchanges that help them inspire change. Therefore, whenever possible, your interactions with them should provide meaningful information and insights about how to help people grow and develop. Given their visionary nature and natural ability to enhance personal relationships, they appreciate enjoyable and fun interactions that focus on future possibilities and are not too detailed.

Understanding dominant quadrant differences is your first step in raising awareness of what you can do to foster relationship harmony. Once you recognize there are differences in perception (i.e., the two of you are operating under different facts and/or beliefs), make an effort to get all perspectives on the table. Differences in perception are known to cause future-versus-now issues. Awareness of your and the other person's time orientation avoids being on different pages regarding the topic being discussed. If you recognize there is a difference in judgment, pay close attention to the thoughts and feelings being expressed. This is when truth versus tact often becomes an issue, so be sure to think carefully before you speak.

Of course, if you are in a blind-spot interaction (meaning your DQs are opposite), pay careful attention to the facts, beliefs, thoughts, and feelings of the person you are interacting with; considerations of future-versus-now orientations; and how you speak in terms of truth versus tact. It is always a good rule of thumb to seek to understand before you attempt to be understood. As you now know, this means understanding the other person's PJs before trying to help them understand yours. The only way to get on the same page in your interactions is to uncover all the facts, beliefs, thoughts, and feelings collectively being held by the two of you.

Exercise 16. Promoting Relationship Harmony

Apply this exercise to a relationship in your life in which you and another person experience conflict. It is likely that you have different or opposite dominant quadrants. Here are the types of comments you might hear describe such relationships:

- I am a naturally spontaneous guy, and she has to plan everything!
- I am the caretaker of our family. He definitely is not!

(Refer to the ACQ Characteristics Table in chapter 1 for more detail.)

Step 1. Be sure you have identified your dominant quadrant and the dominant quadrant of the person with whom you are experiencing conflict. (If needed, refer to chapter 1, exercise 1.) Now document your conflict in your journal.

Step 2. By comparing your DQs, determine where there are differences in perception (sensing or intuition) and/or judgment (thinking or feeling) between the two of you. Can you attribute this conflict to either truth versus tact or future versus now? Are there other differences in facts, beliefs, thoughts, or feelings at work in this relationship? What are they? If needed, refer to cases A through D to support your interaction analysis.

Step 3. Identify the ACQ skill sets you can bolster to increase harmony between you and this person. These are things like tact, truth, time perspective (future versus present), and any LDQ skills that will help you better connect with this person in this situation. Visualize the achievement of a positive outcome using these skills.

For the conflict you are examining, document how you can embrace the other person's dominant quadrant to help you understand his or her perspective. This is not easy to do because it requires you to move out of your comfort zone (your DQ) and into the other person's DQ. However, there is good news. First, by doing this, you develop the skills of an LDQ. Second, if both of you actively and respectfully seek to understand your differences, relationship harmony is achievable. This is true even if just one of you makes the effort. However, harmony is certainly quicker and easier to achieve when you both put effort toward understanding each other's DQ. (You both employ nonjudgmental, seek-to-understand listening and questioning skills.) The bad news is if neither of you attempts to clarify the perceptions and/or judgments driving the disharmony between you, conflict will persist.

Relationship Harmony Key Learning Points

Understanding the behavioral attributes associated with each of the four Authenticity Compass quadrants helps reveal the root cause(s) of interaction conflict in your life. When you find yourself in disagreement with someone, identify the differences that exist in your respective DQs. Accurate awareness of your interacting energy is needed to facilitate harmonious communication. Remember that relationship conflicts are opportunities to increase self-awareness, strengthen active listening, and develop skills associated with your less-dominant quadrants

(LDQs). Ultimately, developing the skills of all four ACQs will increase your interaction effectiveness and enable you to achieve alignment in your relationships.

If you want to communicate in a manner that provides true value to others, you must first take the time to understand what you genuinely believe and think and then choose the best words possible to express your truth. In the context of seeking relationship harmony, think about the following Native American teaching: "It does not require many words to speak the truth" (American Indian Chicago Conference, 1961).

Application 3: The Backward-4 Method for Decision-Making

Conscious decision-making is essential to personal success. The decision-making application called the Backward-4 Method (note: MBTI practitioners refer to this as the Zig-Zag Method) is particularly useful to individuals and groups responsible for solving challenging problems. This proven methodology provides a pathway to a well-thought-out decision or group consensus.[3]

The Backward-4 Method systematically ensures all the facts, beliefs, thoughts, and feelings are examined in a disciplined, inclusive manner before a decision is made. When a person or group faces a difficult decision, the Backward-4 Method minimizes the potential influence of blind spots and ensures the course of action taken is decided consciously. Groups responsible for making a decision benefit from this method because it encourages the perceptions and judgments of all participants to be expressed. The Backward-4 Method guides users to first give attention to the perceiving functions (senses, then intuition) before their attention is given to the judging functions (thoughts, followed by feelings). Said another way, users of this Method evaluate facts first, possibilities second, logical consequences third, and the effect on people last. (See figure 11.)

Figure 11. The Backward-4 Method for Decision-Making

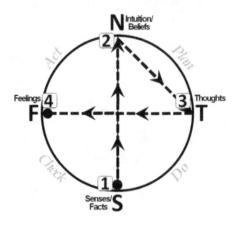

Guideline Questions for Backward-4 Decision-Making

Here are a few questions to serve as a guideline for this decision-making technique:

Facts:

- What are the specifications and constraints involved in this decision?
- What prior experience in this area can be leveraged?

Possibilities:

- What are all the possible solutions?
- Have others employed similar solutions? How do I/we gain access to their experience?

Logical Consequences:

- Is there an existing model or framework to apply?
- What issues, conflicts, or potential setbacks should be considered?

Effect on People:

- What short- and long-term effect will this decision have on the people who will be influenced by it?
- Does this decision support my/our core values?

Here is an example of the Backward-4 Method guiding an individual's decision-making process. It demonstrates the importance of recognizing the influence of one's DQ in decision-making.

An Individual's Decision-Making Example

My grandparents owned and operated a bakery in South Boston, Massachusetts. They named it Alice's Bakery in honor of their first child, my dad's sister, Alice. Being a family enterprise, my father, Arnold, and his four siblings assumed various roles when they were able to properly carry out the tasks associated with these jobs. When my father got his driver's license, he took responsibility for the early-morning bread/donut/pastry deliveries to the bakery's customers in Boston. One morning, after making his first stop, my dad found that the delivery truck would not go into drive, but it would go into reverse (fact-S). He believed (intuition-N) he could make all his deliveries if he drove backward through the city. After thinking through the required route alterations (thoughts-T), he carried out his plan, motivated by his dependable nature and strong sense of responsibility (feelings-F). Driving his truck in reverse, all the deliveries were made on time.

This story not only illustrates how my dad (unknowingly) used the Backward-4 Decision-Making Method but also how his Q3 DQ influenced his problem-solving. He made use of the fact (S) that the truck could move in reverse and was motivated by his feelings (F) of responsibility for his family's business and the needs of its customers. Conversely, if I were in the driver's seat that day instead of my dad, I am certain I would not have made the same decision. My Q1 DQ would have placed a police officer at every street corner, positioned to write me a ticket. This clear mental image would have prevented me from driving backward through the streets of Boston. Instead, it is highly likely that I would have sought help from others.

Given our different DQs (Pam, **Q1**: intuitive thinking, NT/Plan; Arnold, **Q3**: sensing feeling, SF/Check), our respective Backward-4 Decision-Making (SNTF) analyses would probably have looked something like this:

Table 10. SNTF Analysis: DQ Influence on Decision-Making

Pam's SNTF	Arnold's SNTF
S. Truck will only drive in reverse.	**S.** Truck will only drive in reverse.
N. I cannot drive this truck.	**N.** I can drive the truck in reverse without negative consequence.
T. I must find a way to make the deliveries (borrow or rent another vehicle, find a mechanic) or notify customers the reason for my delivery delay.	**T.** I can make the bakery deliveries on time by driving backward.
F. I need help to fix this problem (personally helpless).	**F.** Driving the truck backward will allow me to meet the needs of the bakery's customers and uphold my family's reputation (empowered).

In conclusion, this bakery-delivery story helps explain why different people tend to come up with different solutions for the same problem.

Exercise 17. Decision-Making Using the Backward-4 Method

Step 1. Take out your journal. Identify a current problem or a challenging decision you must make.

Step 2. Jot down the four headings (Facts, Beliefs, Thoughts, and Feelings) and walk through the Backward-4 Method Guideline Questions provided. (If more detail is needed, reference the checklist provided in the SNTF exercise in chapter 4.)

Step 3. Next, consider the following:

- What role is your dominant quadrant playing in this decision?
- If other people are involved, consider the role their DQs are playing.
- What role, if any, are your less-dominant quadrants (LDQs) playing?

Decision-Making Key Learning Points

1. Make optimum use of the Backward-4 Method (SNTF analysis) to ensure structured and comprehensive decision-making takes place. That is to say all facts, beliefs, thoughts, and feelings are put on the table.
2. Recognize that your dominant quadrant tends to steer you toward decisions that optimize your natural strengths.
3. Consider the assistance your LDQs can provide, especially in terms of minimizing your blind spot. Working with people who have a different DQ than you can add new perspectives and valuable insights in problem-solving.

Application 4: ICE-ing (Identify/Cope/Exit-ing)

The Authenticity Compass guides you to success by encouraging your awareness of two essential dynamics: your alignment with the external factors currently defining your existence and your state of personal balance. If you are out of alignment, you cannot experience success. You also will not experience success if, in achieving alignment, you become out of balance with yourself. Therefore, it is essential to both your success and happiness to recognize 1) when you cannot achieve alignment with a specific person or situation no matter how hard you try and 2) when the price of achieving alignment with this person or specific situation is too high because it puts you into a permanent state of imbalance. These are the conditions that position you to ICE.

ICE-ing, an Authenticity Compass acronym for *Identify, Cope, Exit* (escape or eliminate), is a stress management tool designed to be used *with careful consideration*. Understanding and effectively using this application supports your commitment to consciously choosing alignment and balance. The ICE-ing application underscores the fact that sometimes your success and happiness demand that you exit from certain relationships and situations. Here are the defining steps associated with ICE-ing:

Step 1. Identifying the stressor(s) is essential for alignment. It is necessary to identify the underlying root cause(s) of your stress. Start by sitting in quiet, self-reflection. Ask yourself *why* you are in a negative state of being (e.g., sad, angry, fearful, depressed, etc.). Repeat asking yourself why until you exhaust the need to ask. With each answer, document your response in your journal. It is likely this approach will target the root cause(s) of your trouble.

Step 2. Coping is essential for balance. You cope by choosing the most appropriate behavior to deal with the stress, relying on the skills that enable you to do so. To be in balance, you must make sure you are not operating from a blind spot and that you are using skills that effectively address the situation. (Applying the SEE Method and the

PDCA Cycle helps you do this.) This is why developing proficiency with the skills of all four ACQs is essential. Typically, you remain in a state of coping until the situation is resolved or you realize one of the following three scenarios is true:

- You can no longer cope. No matter how hard you try to develop the necessary skills, you just can't.
- You do not want to cope with the situation. This means you have the coping skills, but you do not want to use them. This happens when you become apathetic to the situation and the role you have been playing in it.
- You can cope with the situation, but it is a waste of your energy. Even though you have the required coping skills, your efforts do not (and cannot) bring about positive results. This is because the person (or people) you are coping with have no conscious awareness, intention, desire, or impetus to change their behavior. These are boundary-setting challenges. They teach you not to waste your limited life energy on problems you do not have the power to fix.

Step 3. Exiting (escaping or eliminating) is a choice of last resort. The decision to exit should occur when coping is no longer effective, possible, or tolerable. While life's challenges are the forces that guide your physical, intellectual, emotional, and spiritual growth, you must learn to recognize the situations and relationships where the personal cost associated with your involvement is *detrimental to your well-being*. You should contemplate exiting if you answer no to either of the following questions.

- Can you align with (adequately address) the forces facing you?
- If you can address these forces, can you do so over the time frame required and maintain your balance? For example, my friend was able to take excellent care of his mother for many months until her cancer progressed to the point where her needs became more than he could handle. He had no choice but to bring her to a nursing home.

Exercise 18. Using ICE-ing to Return to Alignment and Balance

1. Think of a life situation (present or past) when the act of coping with stress created personal imbalance. In other words, the cost of alignment and balance was great.
2. Walk through the steps of the ICE application in your journal.
3. What did you learn? Document your insights. What are your next steps?

ICE-ing Key Learning Points

Learning to cope with life's challenges requires skill development. Your Authenticity Compass provides a constant reminder of the four skill areas (defined by the four ACQs) that you need to achieve alignment and balance in life. However, circumstances that require you to stay in a prolonged state of coping can come at too great a price. Staying put in a situation where you cannot maintain personal balance (even after committed skill development on your part) will drain you and, most likely, cause you to become ill. You are too important, and life is too short, for you to allow this to happen.

ICE-ing is a powerful tool that supports choosing to live in personal alignment and balance. It teaches you that sometimes you should end a relationship or leave a situation (such as a poor job fit). This is because not all your choices are about establishing skills to create alignment and balance within your current circumstances. Sometimes, your best choice is to escape from the negative forces you are facing. Realizing a particular challenge requires exiting rather than coping comes with hard-earned self-awareness. May you have the integrity to recognize and the strength to address such challenges when they arise. Most importantly, if you do not have the strength to cope with your life circumstances, please find a qualified mental health professional who will provide the life-affirming guidance you deserve and need.

The ultimate goal of living authentically is to experience well-being. If you feel trapped or stressed out by a job or a relationship, examine the growth opportunities available to you. Identify the skills you are relying upon most heavily. Are they ones supported by your DQ or one of your LDQs? Evaluate your relationship or situation in the context of the PDCA Cycle of Success. Do not sugarcoat or make excuses for what is happening. What facts are you focused on? Are you sure you have all the facts? What are your beliefs about your current situation? Are your beliefs self-limiting? Are you experiencing conflicts of perception or judgment in your interactions with others? Are you operating from a blind spot? Do you need to ICE? The more self-aware you become, the clearer you will be about your life journey. Using the tools and exercises provided in this chapter will help you achieve happiness and success.

Chapter 6 Takeaways

- Using the Authenticity Compass applications will improve your ability to communicate, make decisions, and manage stress. DQ awareness (knowing your dominant quadrant and the DQ of the people with whom you interact) is a prerequisite for the effective use of these four applications.

- *The Blind Spot Management Application* prepares you to effectively respond to challenging circumstances and interactions by alerting you to your potential Authenticity Compass blind spot and the skill development needed to minimize it. (Remember, blind spots are usually located in the quadrant directly opposite of one's DQ.)

- *The Relationship Harmony Application* explains why differences between your DQ and the DQs of others can cause interaction challenges. Awareness of these perception and/or judgment differences (e.g., truth versus tact or future versus now) provides insight into specific communication skills that minimize interpersonal conflict.

- *The Backward-4 Method* is a proven approach for optimal decision-making and problem-solving. This disciplined method is instrumental in achieving group consensus because it uses all related facts, possibilities, thoughts, and feelings of each person involved in determining the solution. Awareness of one's DQ influence is critical when employing the Backward-4 Method.

- *The ICE-ing (Identify, Cope, Exit) Application* provides direction for deciding when it is essential to your well-being to remove yourself from an environment, relationship, or situation because it is not possible for you to establish or sustain a state of personal balance or relationship alignment within it.

- Making conscious choices using awareness of your strengths and skill development opportunities enables you to effectively utilize each of the Authenticity Compass applications to promote alignment and balance in your life.

Our challenge is to match words to deeds
to stop allowing the unacceptable.
—Madeleine Albright

CHAPTER 7
GLOBAL SUCCESS

GLOBAL WELL-BEING REQUIRES GOVERNMENTS, ORGANIZATIONS, and individuals to make aligned and balanced choices based in truth. When human entities consistently make decisions in this way, they have the power to positively influence any system within which they interact. Given that today's global challenges are wide-ranging, interconnected, and increasing in negative effects, it is vital to the well-being of humanity and our planet that every decision, be it private, public, local, national, or international, is made responsibly and with unified intention. The Authenticity Compass supports both individual and group contributions to global success by encouraging self-awareness and guiding the conscious choices that create balance and purposeful alignment. Promoting the strengths of mankind (from a single being to all human society) and the success cycles within and across the systems that bind us, the Authenticity Compass can facilitate the forward motion and cooperation needed to cocreate effective and sustainable global improvement.

This chapter examines key challenges facing humanity, some of the ways these challenges are monitored, and initiatives currently in place to address them. A case is made for the universal adoption of the Authenticity Compass to optimize decision-making, coordinate resources, and accelerate collaboration. The chapter concludes with a discussion of how the Authenticity Compass can address our world's problems, followed by closing thoughts and a call to action.

Worldwide Problems Require Global Solutions

Today's global challenges are growing rapidly and are more complex and interrelated than ever before. Individuals, organizations, and governments (i.e., all human entities) must acknowledge the far-reaching implications of their actions and make choices that lead to global human alignment and balance if mankind is to mitigate the life-damaging threats facing us. For those committed to the creation of a sustainable, healthy, and ethical world, the Authenticity Compass provides direction and support.

An accurate understanding of our global challenges is necessary if we are to combat them. We can turn to the World Economic Forum (WEF), an international, collaborative organization, for its recognized research on global challenges and trends. Five categories of risk are identified in their 2019 *Global Risk Report*[1] and are discussed in terms of likelihood and impact. These include

- societal risks (e.g., water and food crises, rapid and massive spread of infectious disease, and large-scale involuntary migration),
- environmental risks (e.g., extreme weather events, climate action failure, major natural and/or man-made disasters, and loss of biodiversity),
- technological risks (e.g., critical infrastructure breakdown, large-scale cyber attacks, and data fraud/theft),
- economic risks (e.g., financial crises in key economies, failure of critical financial infrastructure or institutions, high unemployment, and illicit trade), and
- geopolitical risks (e.g., weapons of mass destruction, large-scale terrorist attacks, and failure of regional, national, or global governance).

The report underscores the urgency and interconnected nature of these challenges, providing evidence for the cooperation needed to address them. Yet, its authors also pose a critical question: "Is the world sleepwalking into a crisis?"[2] They raise concern over the lack of concerted effort to alleviate these growing challenges when it is clear that conscious awareness and action are more necessary than ever.

Another view of our world's current challenges, The Social Progress Index, is made available by the global nonprofit Social Progress Imperative, which was created in 2010 with direction from professors Scott Sterns of MIT and Michael E. Porter of Harvard.[3] This index, used together with a country's economic measure of gross domestic product (GDP), monitors, prioritizes, and addresses humanity's most pressing issues by providing world, community, and business leaders actionable information by country. Detailed social and environmental measurements of participating countries are gathered and aggregated for comparative and trend analysis. Each country is assigned an overall score based on measures that roll up into the following three areas. (Note: Each of these three areas monitors four specific social progress components.)

1. Basic human needs (nutrition and medical care, water and sanitation, shelter, and personal safety)
2. Foundations of well-being (access to basic knowledge, access to information and communication, health and wellness, and environmental quality)
3. Opportunity to reach full potential (personal rights, personal freedom and choice, inclusiveness, and access to advanced education)

The 2019 Social Progress Index comprises insights from 149 participating countries. The first-place ranking country in 2019 social progress performance is Norway, with an index of 90.95, and the last place (149th) is South Sudan with an index of 24.44.[4] Some other indices of note by place rank include: Germany (eighth), Japan (tenth), the United Kingdom (thirteenth), France (fifteenth), South Korea (twenty-third), the United States (twenty-sixth), Russia (sixty-second), China (eighty-ninth), and Saudi Arabia (ninetieth). While analysts have found a relationship between economic prosperity (GDP per capita) and the social progress of many countries, GDP does not always correlate to social progress performance. This is because factors such as level of investment and priority of resources play defining roles in social progress.

Averaging the Social Progress Index of all 149 countries results in a population-weighted, global index of 64.47. This means the average quality of life across the globe (if the world was a country) falls between that of China and Saudi Arabia. Unfortunately, this 2019 global score has improved only slightly (2.31 points) over the last five years (compared to 2014's global index results). The worldwide performance of the twelve main social progress components driving the global score is mediocre at best. Eight of the twelve components showed modest improvement since 2014's report. However, the world is declining in personal rights and has had no improvement in personal safety, inclusiveness (the lowest scoring global component), or access to basic knowledge. Lack of improvement in the metrics related to individual empowerment (rights, safety, and basic knowledge) and collaboration (inclusiveness) strongly reinforces the need for a worldwide upgrade in social consciousness and action.

To effectively address global challenges, the committed effort of the world's leaders combined with the coordinated management of the world's resources is required. The WEF president, Borge Brende, promotes this concept in the preface of the 2019 WEF Report by stating, "There has never been a more pressing need for a collaborative and multistakeholder approach to shared global problems."[5]

A Framework to Strengthen Global Collaboration

"Global Challenges are transnational in nature and transinstitutional in solution. They cannot be addressed by any government or institution acting alone. They require collaborative action among governments, international organizations, corporations, universities, NGOs, and creative individuals."[6] This quote from the global Millennium Project reinforces the need for all members of our worldwide system (from individual citizens to the largest institutions) to consistently make conscious choices to promote humanity's alignment and balance. Each one of us must learn to respect our true selves and the people with whom we interact if we are to promote harmonious interaction on our planet. The Authenticity Compass provides a means for developing the level of awareness, honesty, and responsibility needed to enable the successful one-to-one, one-to-many, and group-to-group interactions necessary for global success.

Just as individuals each have a unique Authenticity Compass, so do communities, organizations, and governments. The Authenticity Compass provides direction for every human entity (private, public, local, and global) to align with its purpose and strengths, recognize its growth opportunities, and promote its balance. As such, each entity must recognize it is driven by its dominant energy quadrant (its DQ). To optimize and balance its energy and harmoniously align with the entities it depends upon and those who depend upon it, an entity must develop its less-dominant quadrant skills (its LDQs). By learning to optimize the perceptions and judgments that drive conscious choices, leaders can establish and sustain success cycles across the systems that bind our society.

A consistent commitment to conscious choice requires understanding that facts fuel beliefs, beliefs fuel thoughts, and thoughts fuel feelings and actions. It is critical to the alignment and balance of our world that there is a pervasive understanding of these universal drivers of human behavior. Without this awareness, world peace is threatened because people en masse can fall prey to manipulation of these drivers. The radicalizing techniques of extremist groups clearly illustrate that selective data (facts) are used to recruit and influence the beliefs, thoughts, and feelings of members, motivating them to carry out acts of violence. The Spanish Inquisition, the Crusades, the Nazi Holocaust, and the 9/11 attacks are examples of extremism that profoundly underscore humanity's need for global conscious awareness. It is also important to note that mainstream media can be negatively biased and promote fear. A world in which human behavior is based on truth, self-awareness, and responsibility rather than a struggle for power and control must learn the fundamental lessons of these behavior drivers. The Authenticity Compass teaches these lessons. Margareta Drzeniek-Hanouz, a WEF economist, reinforces the importance of these lessons in her statement. "Conflict, whether through cyberattack, competition for resources or sanctions and other economic tools, is broader than ever. Addressing all these possible triggers and seeking to return the world to a path of partnership, rather than competition, should be a priority for leaders."[7]

To meet the rapidly growing challenges facing our planet, it is uplifting to know that there are many initiatives in place around the world advancing positive change, and new initiatives are being created all the time. There is no question that every effort counts. However, given the current likelihood and impact of our global risks, combined with the time pressure of the trends driving them, we should recognize the benefits that would be gained by strengthening initiative alignment:

- When best practices, resources, and plans are shared and leveraged across initiatives, the likelihood of their collective success is greater.
- Initiatives gain positive momentum when the innate strengths of all involved entities offset each other's weaknesses.

Authenticity Compass–driven collaboration is facilitated using the systems-thinking approach needed to implement interdependent cycles of success. This is how cross-functional, cross-initiative improvement opportunities are identified and their achievement accelerated, especially when aided by technologies such as big data analytics.

The United Nations (UN) Foundation, established in 1998, is the largest global organization responsible for setting the world's improvement agenda. In September 2019, the UN Foundation's 193 participating countries created an agenda focused on achieving, by 2030, seventeen Sustainable Development Goals (SDGs). These goals address poverty, inequality, climate, environmental degradation, peace, and justice. Since 2016, the UN Foundation has listed its partners on its website. This list

The Authenticity Compass

is categorized by donors (twelve are listed), foundations and nonprofits (sixty-six), and corporations (102). Considering the volume of partners and the thousands of ongoing worldwide and local initiatives that are not encompassed in the Foundation's collaborative umbrella, it is possible to believe that the SDGs will be achieved by their assigned deadline.

However, even though the Foundation states that it has five core capabilities in place to advance the SDGs (convene, champion, communicate, collaborate, and channel), governance within and across these initiatives seems questionable given the number of partners and nonpartners involved. The Foundation's capabilities depend upon all participants having an accurate understanding of their own core capabilities and also sharing awareness about the existing strengths and weaknesses present within and across each initiative. Adoption of the Authenticity Compass by the people and organizations involved in the SDGs would develop this essential awareness and thereby strengthen the UN Foundation's five core capabilities, ultimately promoting the speed and efficacy of its problem-solving efforts. Here is a high-level overview of how the Authenticity Compass (AC) can bolster the UN Foundation's five core capabilities:

Convene: The AC guides the establishment of effective meeting cycles by ensuring clarity of purpose at both the initiative and participant level and by creating a foolproof process for the ongoing management of each initiative's meeting agendas.

Champion: The AC requires participants to acknowledge, align with, and focus their areas of strength. (The AC is also instrumental in identifying the blind spots and weaknesses of participants that must be addressed to achieve the results desired.)

Communicate: The AC guides successful communication between partners through SNTF awareness, allowing each participant to express their facts, beliefs, thoughts, and feelings. Level setting all SNTFs at the outset ensures decisions are made from a place of full disclosure and understanding.

Collaborate: AC-driven collaboration respects the principles of systems thinking and requires adherence to the PDCA Cycle. Adherence necessitates identifying the interdependencies that exist between and within each cycle. Execution of initiatives using clear communication, feedback, and active listening fosters transparent, effective, and efficient collaboration between related initiatives.

Channel: The AC's support of the above four capabilities facilitates the alignment and balance of each partner's core competencies, strong relationship building, effective decision-making (especially with regard to resource allocation), and avoidance of conflict (or, at the very least, its quick resolution).

The well-being of our planet requires a conscious, concerted effort toward alignment and balance. Because the power of the Authenticity Compass is driven by the proven knowledge that sustainable cycles of success require ongoing relationship building and optimal (aligned and balanced) decision-making based on making the facts (S), beliefs (N), thoughts (T), and feelings (F) of all stakeholders conscious, its universal adoption can streamline global solutions. Developing Authenticity Compass discipline is in the best interest of humanity. By advocating a continuous practice of SNTF-driven decisions, the Authenticity Compass encourages mankind to adopt the altruistic mind-set vital to creating the alignment and balance required for global success.

Consider the Giving Pledge, an inspired initiative developed by Bill and Melinda Gates, Warren Buffett, and other philanthropists in 2010. As a UN Foundation's named partner, the Giving Pledge invites the world's billionaires to commit more than half their wealth to philanthropic and charitable causes during or after their lifetimes. For those who take the pledge, there are opportunities throughout the year to engage in deep discussions about specific topics that benefit society, and there is an annual gathering to share ideas and learn from each other about how best to help the world.

The Giving Pledge is an example of altruistic human behavior and, as such, softens to some degree the concern the father of sociobiology, E. O. Wilson, raises about whether learned altruism in human society is possible.[8] The Giving Pledge brings resources to global challenges. The resources provided by the pledge are critical to the resolution of systemic problems across the planet, but they must be supported with the right interventions (e.g., SNTF consensus and continuously managed PDCA Cycles) if they are to actualize the quickest and best solutions. With a collaborative tool such as the Authenticity Compass, the Giving Pledge and other international initiatives can advance the global mind-set human beings need to thrive.

Using the Authenticity Compass to Improve Nations

Collaboration and leadership accountability is unquestionably necessary to ensure mankind's success. To consistently inspire continuous improvement within our respective countries, communities, and organizations, it is essential that our leaders demonstrate local and global responsibility. It is no longer an option to continue along paths of competitive materialism and greed. Those at the highest levels of society, community, and business must choose to lead our world to a state of sustainable alignment and balance if humanity is to experience global peace and prosperity.

The United States stands out in the Social Progress Index because it is a high-income, leading economy that is in steady social progress decline. Since 2014, the United States has moved from its sixteenth rank position to twenty-sixth place in the overall quality of life for its citizens. Even more sobering than the United States' twenty-sixth-place standing in 2019's Social Progress Index are the underlying scores that determined it. In this report, the United States ranks fifty-ninth in environmental quality, fifty-seventh in personal safety, forty-fifth in access to basic knowledge, and thirty-fourth in health and wellness. A question US citizens and leaders (in government, business, and education) should be asking is: Why is the United States performance so weak in social progress? And, even more importantly: What are we going to do about it? Answers to these questions can be facilitated by examining the nation's Authenticity Compass.

The United States' Authenticity Compass positions it as an ST-driven nation.[9] This means the United States' strength (its dominant energy) is *do*ing and its culture is frequently characterized by the archetype of the sensing-thinking hero. An example of this hero archetype is demonstrated in Rosie the Riveter's message, "We can *do* it," which was used to motivate American women during World War II. More recent examples that promote the United States' DQ include Nike's "Just *do* it" brand marketing campaign and the presidential slogans "Yes we *can*" and "*Make* America great again." The United States' leadership in GDP per capita and its steady focus on production (i.e., *do*ing), especially in the area of defense, reinforces its Q2 dominance. Given this AC Q2 dominance, we also might expect to find weaknesses reflected in its three less-dominant quadrants (LDQs). To explore this hypothesis, ask yourself:

- Are US leaders adequately planning for our country's future? (Q1)
- Are US leaders presently taking good care of our country and people? (Q3)
- Are US leaders inspired to continuously improve the country and its citizens' quality of life? (Q4)

The United States' Social Progress Index provides perspective on the answers to these questions. By bolstering attention in these three LDQ areas, the United States would strengthen alignment with its citizens and most likely improve its lackluster Social Progress Index performance. However, improving its performance issues requires the US government to understand the interdependencies of its challenges. For example, failures related to its infrastructure systems (such as transportation, education, and health care) have created hardships for low-income families for decades.[10] Because underprivileged families rely heavily upon these systems, their failures intensify the distress these families experience and result in a further expansion of the economic inequity that exists between the wealthy and the poor in the United States.

According to research supported by the American Society of Civil Engineers, the health of the train systems in the United States—especially the busiest one in the Northeast corridor—is gravely concerning.[11] Multiple train derailments, causing injury and death, have occurred in the United States from Washington state to New York and Vermont, including a 2015 Amtrak train derailment in Philadelphia that caused the loss of eight lives and more than two hundred injuries. Another transportation example taken from 2015 occurred in Boston, Massachusetts. Snowstorms brought the Massachusetts Bay Transit Authority (the MBTA) to its knees, causing riders, some with infants en route to daycare, to wait hours in bone-chilling weather for alternate transportation. The low-income population, who were dependent on public transportation to get to work during these winter storms, suffered more than any other economic class, and not just because they were forced to endure long hours in the cold. Some also had their pay docked as a result of their tardiness.

The aged US transportation infrastructure, inclusive of its roads, rails, and bridges, requires continuous improvement (Q4 skills)—skills which are associated with the United States' Authenticity Compass's most frequent blind spot. (Q4 is opposite the United States' dominant quadrant). Rosabeth Moss Kanter in her book *Move: Putting America's Infrastructure Back in the Lead*,[12] warns that if America does not fix its failing infrastructure, many cases of avoidable human suffering are certain to occur.

To create positive change in a national system, an all-inclusive stakeholder approach is required. All facts (S), beliefs (N), thoughts (T), and feelings (F) concerning improvement held by stakeholders are taken into account. With this foundation, the success of an improvement process requires ongoing truthful feedback between and within each quadrant of the Authenticity Compass (i.e., each PDCA Cycle step). Depending on scope, existing sub-PDCA Cycles (and their interdependencies) are identified. The Authenticity Compass methodology facilitates optimal decisions by balancing resources and aligning stakeholders according to purpose. Therefore, all systems benefit by using this methodology to guide their design and development (Q1), construction and implementation (Q2), monitoring and maintenance (Q3), and continuous improvement (Q4).

Individuals Are the Heart of Global Success

Like a pebble in a pond, each person's attitudes and actions have a rippling effect on his or her life and the lives of everyone around them. Therefore, it is essential to acknowledge that achieving individual alignment and balance is fundamental to global success. To contemplate the role you play in the achievement of global success, think about your own unique wiring. You are wired for purpose. You hold core beliefs. You filter facts through your belief systems. Your beliefs influence your thinking. Your thinking determines your feelings and behavior. There is only one way to fully engage your wiring. It is to consciously choose to be aligned and balanced.

- *When you are in alignment,* you are positioned to maximize the value you bring to the world, and you consistently make choices to manifest it.
- *When you are in balance,* you are in a state of well-being and are optimally positioned to express your strengths, address your blind spots, and minimize your weaknesses.

Your Authenticity Compass promotes clarity of purpose by guiding you to identify your strengths (your DQ) and your potential growth opportunities (your LDQs) and by encouraging conscious choice in each domain of your life. To achieve your purpose, you must leverage your strengths (the mental functions, behaviors, and skills that come naturally to you) and make a commitment to growth (ongoing skill development). This is what is required to align with your external world, maintain your sense of inner balance, and ultimately achieve flow in your life.

The Authenticity Compass

Because all people are intrinsically connected, your alignment and balance play a critical role in the successful functioning of humanity. Thinking in terms of systems helps you clarify your understanding of the connected nature of everyone. By examining the systems you are a part of (e.g., social, political, economic, religious, educational, familial, etc.), you begin to understand the patterns of behavior you engage in, what forces are influencing you, and the consequences of your behavior. For example, consider a Russian nesting doll as a metaphor for how each individual influences global behavior. Picture yourself as the innermost doll. The second doll out represents your close circle of family and friends. The third doll out represents the community in which you live. The fourth doll encompasses your whole country, and the fifth and outermost doll comprises all people on the planet. If the innermost doll is not balanced and aligned, the outer levels cannot experience alignment and balance. This nesting doll metaphor illustrates the fact that an individual's behavior not only affects those closest to him but also influences his entire system of systems.

Systems thinking underscores the fact that the sustainable success of our planet depends upon the alignment and balance of all human energy. We are each responsible for doing our part to contribute to global well-being. Whether you consider the relationship that exists between two people or two countries, this responsibility demands ongoing commitment to self-awareness and conscious choice. Increasing humanity's conscious awareness and achieving harmonious coexistence requires:

- **Truth:** developing the ability to acknowledge the facts, beliefs, thoughts, and feelings defining our own behavior and narrative and being nonjudgmental of others and ourselves.
- **Responsibility:** making a commitment to our own purpose-driven alignment and balance; living a life defined by conscious choice.
- **Mindfulness:** maintaining awareness of our behavior and choosing to promote balance and alignment within our families, organizations, country, and the world.

Global success is not a fairy tale. It is a mission. Moving forward, every level of society must make a concerted effort to achieve alignment and balance. As R. Buckminster Fuller so aptly states, "We are not going to be able to operate our Spaceship Earth successfully nor for much longer unless we see it as a whole spaceship and our fate as common. It has to be everybody or nobody."[13]

The Authenticity Movement: A Vision for the Future

The following interview with Pamela Bond, the author of *The Authenticity Compass*, enables readers to gain insight into her vision for its universal application.

Q: What inspired you to write *The Authenticity Compass*?

A: *The Authenticity Compass* was inspired by my desire to share key life experiences with my children soon after I was diagnosed with breast cancer. Journaling became a go-to, mind-focusing activity for me. When I realized I had honed in on a functional model for sustainable success at both the individual and organizational level, I felt a strong responsibility to share it with as many people as possible. Writing a book became a logical next step.

Q: Can you explain how *The Authenticity Compass* acts as a functional model for sustainable individual and organizational success?

A: The simplest explanation is that *The Authenticity Compass* leverages two well-established conceptual frameworks that have been used to guide human behavior in personal and business settings for decades. The combined framework (i.e., the Authenticity Compass) explicitly links the concepts of mental function preference with the set of behaviors proven to actualize sustainable goal achievement. It therefore strengthens self-awareness, specifically guiding individuals to better manage their beliefs, thoughts, and feelings, and motivates them to embrace the behavioral changes required to realize their desired outcomes. I have spent many years validating the usefulness of the Authenticity Compass by studying human performance research (in the areas of mental function application and process improvement methodology) and by applying the AC to my life and the lives of those close to me. Users of the Authenticity Compass are empowered by the straightforward behavioral guidance it provides.

Q: How do you envision the Authenticity Compass creating change in the world?

A: I believe the Authenticity Compass offers a unifying communication and problem-solving framework for all people, regardless of their religious, political, or other affiliations and, therefore, can prove instrumental in establishing common ground for solving complex world problems. By developing accountability for our individual SNTFs, the Authenticity Compass encourages honest communication and the perspective that we, the people on this planet, are one connected, single human family. The AC can bring out the best in humanity by instinctively placing urgency on the discussions—in our homes, communities, businesses, and institutions—needed to drive the actions required to ensure humanity's long-term success.

Q: Are there specific sectors or industries that will benefit from the Authenticity Compass? If so, what are they?

A: Given the principles defining the AC apply to all human processes, there isn't a sector or industry that would not benefit from its application. That being said, three areas that are always on the top of my mind are business, technology, and education. Here is a quick overview of the potential role I see the Authenticity Compass playing in each:

The AC can play a major role in the business community, specifically as a framework for advancing the B (benefit) economy and conscious capitalism movements. We have seen leading executives and corporations around the world acknowledge that their focus on maximizing short-term profits and personal compensation has failed and resulted in dire consequences for our world. Many want to move beyond being solely profit-driven to being guided by sustainable business models with social purpose. To achieve this objective, these businesses will need to create and maintain an integrated network of stakeholders (i.e., a system of systems) with fine-tuned, constantly improving success cycles based on clear purpose. This is precisely what the Authenticity Compass is designed to help them deliver.

The technology sector is another area in which Authenticity Compass adoption will prove to be important. Technology advancements have improved our way of life. However, they are advancing so rapidly today that we often find ourselves asking who is benefiting and at what cost. Artificial intelligence (AI) is a prime example of technology that is surrounded by controversy because it is raising a myriad of questions about risk, accountability, and responsibility. I believe the rules for self-learning technologies should be designed with respect for what supports the best in humanity. The Authenticity Compass can guide technologists to design AI algorithms that actualize sustainable cycles of success and, at the same time, cultivate the character strengths of humanity (e.g., love, curiosity, gratitude, and hope).

Lastly, I see the Authenticity Compass playing a pivotal role in education. We have been witnessing a promising shift in the ethos of the last few generations. For example, millennials are generally honest, significantly less focused on materialism, and believe in the sustainability message. By teaching the Authenticity Compass in schools, children could learn to become self-aware at a young age. My vision is that by the time students graduate from high school, they would 1) understand their unique strengths, 2) have learned how to achieve personal alignment and balance, and 3) know how to make conscious choices that support their purpose in life. The adage that we are placing the future of our planet in the hands of our children is a powerful one to think about. It is up to us to give our children the tools they need to be successful. This belief directly links back to why I wrote *The Authenticity Compass* in the first place.

People who use the AC to improve their lives and pursue their purpose positively influence everyone around them. The rippling effect of freeing oneself from limiting beliefs and negative patterns of behavior creates a contagious, positive shift in thoughts, feelings, and actions. I ask you to think about the implications of this shift in your interactions with others. If you do, you will participate in a bottom-up authenticity movement and encourage our collective ability to ensure the well-being of mankind and the planet. The future of humanity is counting on us to do so.

Closing Thoughts and a Call to Action

Every person has a role in the success of Earth's well-being. As such, you have a responsibility to yourself, humankind, and the planet to live out your purpose and your full potential. By raising your awareness and making conscious choices for alignment and balance, you create a resonance of harmony that influences humanity. Whether you manage a home, a small business, a major corporation, or a government, you are responsible for the energy that you create. When you maintain balance and are in alignment with your purpose and world, you encourage positive flow throughout the systems within which you operate. Your contribution of positive energy supports global success.

Earth is a unified system of essential natural resources. One man's need to breathe fresh air and drink clean water is the same need all people have. The threats to human life, such as climate change, weapons of mass destruction, and biological pandemics (e.g., COVID-19), affect all people equally no matter their socioeconomic status or where they live on the planet. While the number of initiatives currently in place to address these threats is encouraging, more must be done to improve our preparedness and response.

The good news is that today's technology can support large-scale analysis and better information sharing than in any previous time in history. Initiatives such as the Social Development Goals and the Giving Pledge demonstrate sincere commitment to fixing the world's problems.

However, will these efforts be sufficient for the ongoing stewardship of our planet? I contend that they just might be if a consistent global mind-set—a unifying framework for conscious universal dialogue—is established. The Authenticity Compass provides such a framework by guiding its users to leverage each other's strengths and minimize each other's weaknesses. To advance human consciousness and actualize global unity, we must cocreate cycles of success by continually learning from our collective efforts to achieve alignment and balance. The Authenticity Compass can guide this learning

Referencing the nesting doll metaphor, we can visualize world peace as an extrapolation of individual peace. The following sentence, taken from a Christian hymn, is a reminder of the role we each play on the world stage: "Let there be peace on Earth, and let it begin with me."

It is not a coincidence that all religions provide the same foundational guidance for peace. Jeffrey Moses highlights this fact in his book *Oneness*[14] by showing us that the Golden Rule, a basic principle for optimum human behavior, is expressed in the scriptures of every religion, almost word for word, as shown in the following table.

Table 11. The Universal Golden Rule

Religion	The Golden Rule[15]
Christianity	Do unto others as you would have them do unto you.
Judaism	What is hurtful to you, do not do to other people.
Islam	Do unto all men as you would they should unto you.
Buddhism	Hurt not others with that which pains yourself.
Hinduism	Treat others as thou wouldst thyself be treated.

The Golden Rule, when considered in the context of groups, such as communities and countries, takes on an even deeper meaning. Edward O. Wilson's book, *The Meaning of Human Existence*, compares the concepts of group altruism with survival of the fittest in terms of their influence on man's survival. His critical message is that while "selfish members win within groups ... groups of altruists succeed over groups of selfish members."[16] This means that while a selfish individual may win the most resources, the groups they are a part of will not exist as well or as long as the ones whose members are concerned about the welfare of each other. Wilson makes his readers question whether the human race can embrace altruism in a world where most religious, political, economic, and other pressures reinforce tribal-like competitiveness rather than global unity. This then begs the often-pondered question: Can man live by the Golden Rule? I believe most people, if asked, would agree that man's survival demands these questions be answered with a resounding *yes*. A quote from Mildred Lisette Norman (aka the Peace Pilgrim) strongly supports this belief: "We are all cells in the same body of humanity." We are each dependent upon each other in ways similar to how the brain relies on the lungs for oxygen and the bloodstream relies on the heart for its circulation.[17]

You are a member of a global community. As such, I sincerely hope you join me in the creation of an authenticity movement. By committing to the ongoing awareness of your perceptions, your judgments, and the patterns of behavior defining your life, you will learn to create and maintain cycles of success. By doing so, you will live your purpose and actively participate in the conscious evolution of humanity. For the sake of present and future generations, please accept this invitation to use your Authenticity Compass to become your best self and contribute your gifts to the world. By consciously choosing to align and balance your physical, spiritual, mental, and emotional energy, you will embrace your true power, experience personal success and well-being, and contribute to the survival of our planet.

The next step in human evolution is not inevitable, but for the first time in the history of our planet, it can be a conscious choice. Who is making that choice? YOU are.
—Eckhart Tolle

Your beliefs become your thoughts,
Your thoughts become your words,
Your words become your actions,
Your actions become your habits,
Your habits become your values,
Your values become your destiny.
—Mahatma Gandhi

NOTES

Chapter 1. Authenticity Compass Basics

1. Charles Martin, *Looking at Type: The Fundamentals* (Gainesville, FL: Center for Applications of Psychological Type, 1997), 8.

2. Gregory E. Huszczo, *Making a Difference by Being Yourself: Using Your Personality Type at Work and in Relationships* (Mountain View, CA: Davies-Black Publishing, 2009), 27.

3. Gordon D. Lawrence, *Finding the Zone: A Whole New Way to Maximize Mental Potential* (Amherst, NY: Prometheus Books, 2010), 91.

4. Lawrence, 4.

5. Lawrence, 4.

6. Lawrence, 5.

7. Lawrence, 5.

8. Huszczo, *Making a Difference by Being Yourself*, 27.

9. Huszczo, 27.

10. Huszczo, 27.

11. Huszczo, 27.

Chapter 2. Alignment

1. John Geirland, "Go With The Flow," *Wired Magazine*, September 1996, 1–2.

2. The American Institute of Stress, "What is Stress?" January 4, 2017, www.stress.org.

3. Lyle H. Miller, Robert Ross, and Sanford I. Cohen, "STRESS: What Can Be Done? A Guide to Reducing the Strain Caused by Mismanaged Stress," *Bostonia Magazine* 56 (1982), 37–48.

Chapter 3. Balance

1. Sonja Lyubomirsky and Jamie Kurtz, *The How of Happiness: A New Approach to Getting the Life You Want* (New York: Penguin Books, 2007), 15.

2. Bob Greene, *The Life You Want: Get Motivated, Lose Weight, and Be Happy* (New York: Simon & Schuster, 2010), 211.

3. Alberto Villoldo, *The Four Insights: Wisdom, Power, and Grace of the Earthkeepers* (Carlsbad, CA: Hay House, 2006), 98.

Chapter 4. Choice

1. Harvard Health Publishing, "Understanding the Stress Response," Harvard University, updated May 2018, www.health.harvard.edu/staying-healthy/understanding-the-stress-response.

2. Paul D. Tieger and Barbara Barron-Tieger, *Do What You Are: Discover the Perfect Career for You Through the Secrets of Personality Type* (New York: Little, Brown and Company, 2001), 87.

3. Carolyn Myss, *Sacred Contracts: Awakening Your Divine Potential* (New York: Three Rivers Press, 2003), 14–16.

4. Lyubomirsky and Kurtz, *The How of Happiness*, 22.

5. Elisabeth Kubler-Ross, *On Death and Dying* (New York: Macmillan Publishing, 1969), 11–37.

6. Eckhart Tolle, *The Power of Now: A Guide to Spiritual Enlightenment* (Novato, CA: Namaste Publishing and New World Library, 1999).

7. Eckhart Tolle, *A New Earth: Awakening to Your Life's Purpose* (New York: Penguin Books, 2005).

8. Viktor E. Frankl, *Man's Search for Meaning* (New York: Pocket Books, 1984).

9. Don Miguel Ruiz, *The Four Agreements: A Practical Guide to Personal Freedom (A Toltec Wisdom Book)* (San Rafael, CA: Amber-Allen Publishing, 1997).

10. Kubler-Ross, *On Death and Dying*, 181–244.

11. Wayne Dyer, *Excuses Begone: How to Change Lifelong, Self-Defeating Thinking Habits* (Carlsbad, CA: Hay House, 2009), 10.

12. A. Ortony and T.J. Turner, "What's Basic About Basic Emotions?" *Psychological Review* 97 (1990): 315–31.

13. W. Edwards Deming, *Out of the Crisis* (Cambridge, MA: Massachusetts Institute of Technology, Center for Advanced Engineering Study, 1992), 86–96.

Chapter 5. Personal Success

1. Kristen Sturt, "The Surprising Link between Longevity and Volunteering: Here's Why Your Giving Season Should Last All Year," May 3, 2019, www.considerable.com.
2. Ryan M. Niemic and Robert E. McGrath, *The Power of Character Strengths: Appreciate and Ignite Your Positive Personality* (VIA Institute on Character, 2019), 26–27.
3. Jane S. Anderson, *30 Days of Character Strengths: A Guided Practice to Ignite Your Best* (Strength Based Living, 2018).

Chapter 6. Authenticity Compass Applications

1. Carolyn Zeisset, *The Art of Dialogue: Exploring Personality Differences for More Effective Communication* (Gainesville, FL: Center for Applications of Psychological Type, 2006), 103–13.
2. Zeisset, *The Art of Dialogue,* 104.
3. Zeisset, 83–85.

Chapter 7. Global Success

1. World Economic Forum, "The Global Risk Report, Fourteenth Edition," (Geneva: World Economic Forum, 2019), 97–98, www.weforum.org.
2. World Economic Forum, *The Global Risk Report*, 6.
3. Michael Porter, "Why Social Progress Matters," *Project Syndicate*, April 2015.
4. Social Progress Imperative, "2019 Social Progress Index Executive Summary V2.0," 2019, 6–7, www.socialprogress.org.
5. World Economic Forum, *The Global Risk Report*, 5
6. The Millennium Project, "Global Futures Studies & Research: 15 Global Challenges," 2017, www.millennium-project.org.

7. Margareta Drzenick-Hanouz, "International Conflict Biggest Threat to Global Stability," January 15, 2015, www.economictimes.com.

8. Edward O. Wilson, *The Meaning Of Human Existence* (New York: Liveright Publishing Corporation, 2014), 189–201.

9. Carol Pearson, "Organization and Team Culture Indicator Instrument Qualifying Training" (qualification program, Hampton Inn Suites, Arlington, VA, September 22–24, 2004).

10. Robert Putnam, *Our Kids: The American Dream in Crisis* (New York: Simon & Schuster, 2015), 221–36.

11. Irwin Redliner, "How Congress Caused the Amtrak Crash," *The Daily Beast*, May 15, 2015, thedailybeast.com.

12. Rosabeth Moss Kanter, *Move: Putting America Infrastructure Back in the Lead*, 12–3.

13. "R. Buckminster Fuller Quotes," Brainy Quote, accessed January 21, 2019, BrainyQuote.com/quotes/r_buckminster_fuller_153429.

14. Jeffrey Moses, *Oneness: Great Principles Shared By All Religions* (New York: Ballantine Books, 2002), 5.

15. Moses, 5.

16. Edward O. Wilson, *The Meaning Of Human Existence*, 63–179.

17. Mildred Lisette Norman, *Charter for Compassion*, accessed December 5, 2019, www.charterforcompassion.org/mildred-lisette-norman-ryder-peace-pilgrim.

BIBLIOGRAPHY

The American Institute of Stress. "What Is Stress?" January 4, 2017. www.stress.org.

Anderson, Jane S. *30 Days of Character Strengths: A Guided Practice to Ignite Your Best.* Strength Based Living, 2018.

Brown, Brené. *I Thought It Was Just Me (But It Isn't): Making the Journey from "What Will People Think?" to "I Am Enough."* New York: Avery, 2007.

Corlett, John G. and Carol S. Pearson. *Mapping the Organizational Psyche: A Jungian Theory of Organizational Dynamics and Change.* Gainesville, FL: Center for Applications of Psychological Type, 2003.

Deming, W. Edwards. *Out of the Crisis.* Cambridge, MA: Massachusetts Institute of Technology Center for Advanced Engineering Study, 1992.

Drzenick-Hanouz, Margareta. "International Conflict Biggest Threat to Global Stability." January 15, 2015. www.economictimes.com.

Dyer, Wayne. *Excuses Begone.* Carlsbad, CA: Hay House, 2009.

Frankl, Viktor E. *Man's Search for Meaning.* New York: Pocket Books, 1984.

Fuller, R. Buckminster. Brainy Quote. BrainyQuote.com/quotes/r_buckminster_fuller_153429.

Geirland, John. "Go With The Flow." *Wired Magazine,* September 1996.

Greene, Bob. *The Life You Want: Get Motivated, Lose Weight, and Be Happy.* New York: Simon & Schuster, 2010.

Harvard Health Publishing. "Understanding the Stress Response." Harvard University. Updated May 1, 2018. www.health.harvard.edu/staying-healthy/understanding-the-stress-response.

Huszczo, Gregory E. *Making a Difference by Being Yourself: Using Your Personality Type at Work and in Relationships.* Mountain View, CA: Davies-Black Publishing, 2009.

Kanter, Rosabeth Moss. *Move: Putting American Infrastructure Back in the Lead.* New York: W.W. Norton & Company, 2015.

Kubler-Ross, Elisabeth. *On Death and Dying.* New York: Macmillan Publishing, 1969.

Lawrence, Gordon D. *Finding the Zone: A Whole New Way to Maximize Mental Potential.* Amherst, NY: Prometheus Books, 2010.

Lyubomirsky, Sonja and Jamie Kurtz. *The How of Happiness: A New Approach to Getting the Life You Want.* New York: Penguin Books, 2007.

Mackey, John and Raj Sisodia. *Conscious Capitalism: Liberating the Heroic Spirit of Business.* Boston: Harvard Business Review Press, 2014.

Martin, Charles. *Looking at Type: The Fundamentals.* Gainesville, FL: Center for Applications of Psychological Type, 1997.

Miller, Lyle H., Robert Ross, and Sanford I. Cohen. "STRESS: What Can Be Done? A Guide to Reducing the Strain Caused by Mismanaged Stress." *Bostonia Magazine* 56, 1982.

Moses, Jeffrey. *Oneness: Great Principles Shared By All Religions.* New York: Ballantine Books, 2002.

Myss, Carolyn. *Sacred Contracts: Awakening Your Divine Potential*. New York: Three Rivers Press, 2003.

Niemic, Ryan M., and Robert E. McGrath. *The Power of Character Strengths: Appreciate and Ignite Your Positive Personality*. VIA Institute on Character, 2019.

Norman, Mildred Lisette. Charter for Compassion. Accessed December 5, 2019: www.charterforcompassion.org/mildred-lisette-norman-ryder-peace-pilgrim.

Ortony, A., and T.J. Turner. "What's Basic about Basic Emotions?" *Psychological Review* no. 97, 1990.

Pearson, Carol. "Organization and Team Culture Indicator Instrument Qualifying Training." Qualifying program at Hampton Inn Suites, Arlington, VA, September 22–24, 2004.

Porter, Michael. "Why Social Progress Matters." *Project Syndicate*, April 2015.

Putnam, Robert. *Our Kids: The American Dream in Crisis*. New York: Simon & Schuster, 2015.

Redliner, Irwin. "How Congress Caused the Amtrak Crash." *The Daily Beast*, May 15, 2015. www.thedailybeast.com.

Ruiz, Don Miguel. *The Four Agreements: A Practical Guide to Personal Freedom*. San Rafael, CA: Amber-Allen Publishing, 1997.

Social Progress Imperative. "2019 Social Progress Index Executive Summary V2.0." 2019. www.socialprogress.org.

Sturt, Kristen. "The Surprising Link between Longevity and Volunteering: Here's Why Your Giving Season Should Last All Year." May 3, 2019. www.considerable.com.

The Millennium Project. "Global Futures Studies & Research: 15 Global Challenges." 2017. www.millennium-project.org.

Tieger, Paul D., and Barbara Barron-Tieger. *Do What You Are: Discover the Perfect Career for You through the Secrets of Personality Type.* New York: Little, Brown and Company, 2001.

Tolle, Eckhart. *The Power of Now.* Novato, CA: Namaste Publishing and New World Library, 1999.

Tolle, Eckhart. *A New Earth: Awakening to Your Life's Purpose.* New York: Penguin Books, 2005.

Villoldo, Alberto. *The Four Insights: Wisdom, Power, and Grace of the Earthkeepers.* Carlsbad, CA: Hay House, 2006.

Wilson, Edward O. *The Meaning of Human Existence.* New York: Liveright Publishing Corporation, 2014.

World Economic Forum. "The Global Risks Report 14th Edition." Geneva: World Economic Forum. 2019. www.weforum.org.

Zeisset, Carolyn. *The Art of Dialogue: Exploring Personality Differences for More Effective Communication.* Gainesville, FL: Center for Applications of Psychological Type, 2006.

ABOUT THE AUTHOR

BOSTON NATIVE AND GIRL'S LATIN School graduate Pamela Bond has a broad range of experience developing innovative business processes and creating world-class service strategies. Her career spans the disciplines of medical and biobehavioral research, software engineering, corporate planning, and management consulting. Bond is a skilled facilitator and lecturer whose last corporate role was the VP of customer experience for Fidelity Investments. She is certified in positive psychology from the Wholebeing Institute, is a qualified administrator of the Myers-Briggs Type Indicator, and is a member of the Institute of Coaching affiliated with Harvard Medical School. She holds a master of science in information management from Northeastern University and a bachelor of science in biology from the University of Massachusetts. Bond cherishes her husband, daughter, son, stepdaughter, and grandchildren. Their love provides her with a constant source of happiness, strength, and motivation. Bond and her husband live close to Boston in order for her to have easy access to excellent medical care and to regularly enjoy the ocean's beauty.

NOTE FROM THE AUTHOR

I AM HAPPY TO HEAR from readers, especially people who want assistance in learning how to optimally use their Authenticity Compass. To reach me please send a message to pamela.bond.m@gmail.com. I will respond to you as quickly as I am able.

CPSIA information can be obtained
at www.ICGtesting.com
Printed in the USA
LVHW030101080821
694192LV00001B/27